SHENANDOAH UNIVERSITY LIBRARY
WINCHESTER, VA 22601

D1778904

Mark Twain and Religion

American University Studies

Series XXIV
American Literature
Vol. 9

PETER LANG
New York • Bern • Frankfurt am Main • Paris

John Q. Hays

Mark Twain and Religion

A Mirror of American Eclecticism

edited by
Fred A. Rodewald

PETER LANG
New York • Bern • Frankfurt am Main • Paris

Library of Congress Cataloging-in-Publication Data

Hays, John Q.
  Mark Twain and religion : a mirror of American eclecticism / John Q. Hays ; edited by Fred A. Rodewald.
    p. cm.—(American university studies. Series XXIV, American literature ; vol. 9)
  Includes index.
  1. Twain, Mark, 1835-1910 — Religion. 2. Religion in literature. I. Rodewald, Fred A. II. Title.
  III. Series.
  PS1342.R4H34   1989   818'.409—dc19   88-13553
  ISBN 0-8204-0854-9   CIP
  ISSN 0895-0512

CIP-Titelaufnahme der Deutschen Bibliothek

Hays, John Q.:
Mark Twain and religion : a mirror of American eclecticism / John Q. Hays. Ed. by Fred A. Rodewald. — New York; Bern; Frankfurt am Main; Paris: Lang, 1988.
  (American University Studies: Ser. 24, American Literature; Vol. 9)
  ISBN 0-8204-0854-9

NE: American University Studies / 24

```
PS             Hays, John Q.
1342
.R4            Mark Twain and
H34              religion
1989
818 T911ha
```

© Peter Lang Publishing, Inc., New York 1989

All rights reserved.
Reprint or reproduction, even partially, in all forms such as microfilm, xerography, microfiche, microcard, offset strictly prohibited.

Printed by Weihert-Druck GmbH, Darmstadt, West Germany

for Rene

TABLE OF CONTENTS

Introductory Note	ix
Acknowledgments	xv
Chapter I	1
Chapter II	17
Chapter III	43
Chapter IV	65
Chapter V	85
Chapter VI	121
Chapter VII	151
Chapter VIII	179
Chapter IX	219
Index	223

INTRODUCTORY NOTE

Like the Sirens's song, the Dream enticed the first Europeans to North America, and recurrences of it lured here succeeding generations from all continents. Typified by Coronado's futile search for <u>Cibola</u>, the legendary seven cities with streets paved of gold, Spanish Conquistadores and their accompanying Catholic priests responded to the material and spiritual appeals of the Dream. They marched under the banners of <u>Dios y oro</u> (God and gold) and sought to Christianize the native Indians and to appropriate the reputed wealth of their lands. Later, the Massachusetts Bay Colony's Protestant English Puritans aspired to build what Winthrop called a city "on a hill" or a "New Zion," celebrating the spiritual but also rejoicing in the material blessings of an intervening God. Finally, the Dream acquired a third and last appeal: the fruits of political independence from British, French, and Spanish monarchial rule.

Whetting the pursuit of the triadic Dream for freed Americans and for immigrants, the frontier of the trans-Mississippi West beckoned with free land to be claimed for farming and ranching and with mineral wealth to be extracted from the earth. "It was westering and westering," Steinbeck's leader of the people called the appeals and the response. And hordes of Dreamers raced after it, oblivious of the failure of the "New Zion" from compromise such as the Half-Way Covenant and from the challenges of the Enlightenment; unmindful of the fact that instant wealth had failed to be bestowed gratuitously upon Everyman; and forgetful that many of the freedoms offered by the new nation did not extend originally to men and women slaves, all other women, and persons without property--that is, to persons ignored or sacrificed to political expediency at the birth of the republic.

Eventually, the Dream led the Dreamers to the shores of the vast Pacific Ocean; and, in its earth-bound form, westering necessarily stopped. The barrier represented by the Pacific symbolized the inherent weakness of the Dream. Despite the fact that dreams all reside on the abstract heights of perfection, the dreamers must labor in the land-locked reality of imperfection. <u>Cibola</u>, therefore, must continually fade into the distance beyond the outstretched hands of Coronado's children even though it may tantalize them with a few gold coins sprinkled along their paths. The peal of bells from the "New Zion" may herald yet another sabbath but not the Millennium. And our political institutions may offer freedom in larger measures than ever before but must withhold the final measure lest freedom become license.

Himself sometimes a Dreamer as was his father, Mark Twain carefully observed the pursuits of the Dream during his lifetime, which bridged the frontier and the Age of Science just as it did the untamed West and the more refined East. His essays, novels, and stories frequently concerned religion, materialism, and politics. Those dealing with religion have attracted particular scholarly interest. From A. B. Paine to the present, scholars created and elaborated what might be termed a biographical and critical dogma: that Twain, aggrieved by the deaths of his wife and three of their four children and financially distressed by bad investments, became increasingly pessimistic, deterministic, and even contradictory in his writing. A related canon of the dogma has been that Twain also suffered from the suspicion he had failed artistically.

What scholarship has failed to perceive is that, realistically faithful to his observations, Twain mirrored the weaknesses inherent in the American religious Dream more so than revealed his personal inward struggles. Searching for an expanded understanding of the creative force and man's relationship to it, Americans successively examined Roman Catholic and Protestant Christianity, with its Judaic and Hellenistic backgrounds; Deism (and its kindred strands of Unitarianism and Transcendentalism, the latter with some Oriental affiliations); evolutionary Naturalism; and scientific Determinism. As pragmatists, they retained useful old concepts as they embraced new so that the result overall was eclectic and naturally pessimistic, deterministic, and contradictory. The inconsistencies of such eclecticism, however, scarcely troubled the seekers. As Whitman said in a related context: "Do I contradict myself? Very Well, then, I contradict myself./ I am large, I contain multitudes."

Similarly, in writing about those concepts, as well as the

folkloric supernaturalism of the black slaves he knew in his youth, Twain is necessarily pessimistic, deterministic, and contradictory. And that is the plight of all earth-bound writers dealing with abstractions. The best they can hope to do, as St. Paul said, is to see through a glass "darkly" and then, as Huck Finn declared that Twain had done, to tell the truth "mainly" or incompletely and perhaps even obliquely.

Perceiving what scholarship to his time had failed to grasp about Twain's religious writing, Professor John Q. Hays set out near the end of his distinguished academic career to correct the oversight. His interest in Twain was natural. Like Twain, Hays was born in the Mississippi River Valley but in neighboring Arkansas rather than in Twain's native Missouri; and, more significantly, like Twain and most other Southern writers, he acquired an intense devotion to home-place. He matriculated at the University of Missouri, earning baccalaureate and master's degrees and emphasizing the study of American literary Realism with Twain's writing as a focal point. For his doctoral dissertation at Berkeley, Hays wrote about Twain. Continued study gave Hays encyclopedic knowledge both of primary and secondary sources and acute critical insights that enhanced his university teaching career both domestically and, as a Fulbright lecturer, at the University of South Africa in Cape Town.

Shortly before his sudden death in Austria, where he had been retracing part of a route Twain himself once followed, Hays completed the first draft of the manuscript of this book. His widow Rene resolved to carry on the unfinished project and enlisted the assistance of Professor Fred A. Rodewald. Rodewald had studied under Hays at Texas A&M University and then had served with him as a faculty member at Stephen F. Austin State University, where Hays had completed his career as a teacher and a publishing scholar. Bringing an understanding of Hay's bent of mind to the project, Rodewald added his own considerable knowledge both of Twain and American Realism and his own writing style refined by published scholarly articles and creative works. The work of Hays and Rodewald, as this book has become, properly restores Twain to the more eminent position from which his literary reputation had fallen as a result of the earlier scholarly dogmatism.

--Edwin W. Gaston, Jr., Emeritus
Stephen F. Austin State University

ACKNOWLEDGMENTS

The author and the editor of this book have incurred obligations in the course of their research and writing. For the late John Q. Hays and himself, the editor herewith and gratefully acknowledges the generous contributions of the following persons:

(1) Rene Hays, whose devotion to the cause has brought this book to fruition;

(2) The librarians of the R. W. Steen Library, Stephen F. Austin State University, for research assistance;

(3) The administration of Stephen F. Austin State University for financial and other assistance; and

(4) Davalyn Fleniken Lapp, Kathy Lunsford and English Department staff whose good nature and skills in computerized typesetting produced the manuscript.

-- Fred A. Rodewald

CHAPTER 1: INTRODUCTION

Since his death in April 1910, many scholars and critics have maintained that Samuel Clemens (Mark Twain) ended his career in bleak despair.[1] Most of the responsibility for this myth belongs to Albert Bigelow Paine, who wrote the massive multi-volume authorized Clemens's biography. His firsthand account of Clemens's last decade when Paine knew him takes up a third of the biography's 1719 pages, but for his account of Clemens's early life, Paine relied heavily upon two sources, less than unimpeachable. The first was Clemens himself, plagued by an admittedly erratic memory and a habit of exaggeration sometimes whetted by his Boswellian recorder's gullibility. The second was neighborhood old-timers in Missouri and elsewhere who provided authentic data mixed with hearsay about a town's young scapegrace and "one-gallus lad" who became a national figure. To Paine, young Sam Clemens was dominated by a pious Calvinistic mother whose home teaching convinced him that "Flames were being kept brisk for little boys who were heedless of sacred matters."[2] The elder Clemens, according to Paine, ceased to believe in the Scriptures but clung to a Calvinistic spirit.

Paine's simplified account of Clemens's Calvinistic background was given greater acceptance in the 1920's by Van Wyck Brooks whose moral lecture in The Ordeal of Mark Twain (1920) virtually patented the myth of Clemens's despair. Brooks did not have available to him the bulk of Twain's later work, but neither was he well acquainted with nor sympathetic toward the writings of Twain's Western apprenticeship. He drew heavily upon Paine's biography and was unabashedly influenced by a book he failed to acknowledge anywhere within his own--Bernard Hart's The Psychology of Insanity (1912), "a synthesis of four schools of psychological thought--Freud's, Janet's, Adler's, Jung's" upon which he patterned his analysis of Clemens's psychic experience.[3] Brooks, taking Clemens's despair to be the gospel truth, asserted that one of the most bountifully endowed of America's writers wound up a frustrated, bitter pessimist because of a childhood conflict between his will and his unconscious desire to create. The will was formed by the influence of Clemens's puritanical instruction at home and later reinforced by the Gilded Age philosophy: "Be good and you will succeed in business." According to Brooks, the will won out over Clemens's creative "unconscious self" that could fulfill itself "only through the life of the artist."[4]

In 1932 with his Mark Twain's America, Bernard DeVoto set out to squash the claims of Brooks. DeVoto not only found Brooks humorless, he knew from first-hand experience and data that Brooks was completely wrong in describing frontier America as sterile soil "for the seed of genius to fall in," and he deplored critics Mumford and Josephson's acceptance of Brooks's thesis.[5] Then follows an odd development in Twainian scholarship bearing directly on the myth of Clemens's despair. Whether intentionally or not, DeVoto documented Brooks's chief accusation that Clemens ended up a bitter pessimist. In Clemens's boyhood, DeVoto said, when an invigorating spirit labelled Manifest Destiny permeated the Western frontier, young Sam Clemens and his generation were imbued with the hope of a New Jerusalem. By the century's end the simple rural world that shaped the youngster had been transformed by science and technology into an urban, industrialized society too complex for the mature Clemens to understand. As a sensitive America-watcher, Clemens witnessed his beloved country drifting toward materialism and imperialism, evil and anti-democratic destinations. And Christianity, whose moral implications Clemens in his idiosyncratic way had preached throughout his career, was become a sham by acting as a full-time partner in the process. "In intellectual terms," concludes DeVoto, Clemens "had experienced the intent of his age and its reality. I cannot see in his pessimism anything but the fruit of his experience."[6] DeVoto codified his rationale for Clemens's despair in <u>Mark Twain in America</u> (1940) and in <u>Mark Twain at Work</u> (1942) after examining the voluminous Mark Twain papers.

But if DeVoto called into question conclusions drawn by Brooks, his own inferences have occasionally proven suspect. For one thing, to verify and authenticate his conclusions about Clemens's final despair, DeVoto used the edition of <u>The Mysterious Stranger</u> (1916) which Paine and Frederick A. Duneka, then manager of Harper and Brothers, collaborated on, an edition which John S. Tuckey found to contain enough editorial changes to warrant being called "a collaborative creation" or the work of co-authors.[7] Other scholars and investigators have attempted to substantially correct the Paine-Brooks oversimplifications. Clemens's grandnephew Samuel Charles Webster drew upon family materials in editing <u>Mark Twain: Business Man</u> (1946) and Minnie Brashear, Alexander E. Jones, and Dixon Wecter steeped themselves in the Hannibal period of Clemens's life, gleaning first-hand evidence unavailable to Paine or Brooks. But in spite of their contributions, the myth of Clemens's final despair persists. Justin Kaplan sparked the renewal of the old controversy when he remarked in his critical biography <u>Mr. Clemens and Mark Twain</u> (1966) that Clemens "remained an unbeliever,"[8] a charge that brought out a defense by Clemens's distant relative Cyril Clemens,[9] and John T. Frederick said in 1969 that Clemens's final say in religion was "absolute negation . . . nihilism."[10] Perhaps it is now possible to understand where the welter of critical opinion and evidence has left us and to see that early and late Clemens was a man of immensely eclectic religious views.

Early criticism accepted Van Wyck Brook's notion that Samuel Clemens's mother Jane was a dour stiff-necked Calvinist primarily responsible for her famous son's final pessimism. Jane Clemens's granddaughter, Annie Moffett Webster, who lived with her grandmother Clemens for twenty-five years, claimed the Brooks portrait totally false.[11] Dixon Wecter pointed out that far from being the fire-and-brimstone type of Presbyterian, Jane Clemens was quite tolerant of all religions and at the age of forty encouraged her daughter Pamela to take her choice between either the Presbyterian or the Methodist churches. Wecter cites Jane Clemens's pastor at this time recalling "Sister Clemens" as the very opposite of dour and stiff-necked.[12] Such claims do not prove that Sam Clemens was immune to a Calvinist influence or that his mother and other family members did not influence his attitude toward religion, but they do indicate that whatever Calvinism shows up in Sam's view of the world must be attributed to sources other than his luke-warmly pious mother, who is reported to have said on one occasion, "I know that a person that can turn his cheek is higher and holier than I am . . . but I despise him, too, and wouldn't have him for a doormat."[13] Not only was Brooks wrong about Jane Clemens, he failed to see what recent scholarship has amply demonstrated, that Sam Clemens's youth was spent in a welter of diverse religious opinion and belief that probably had a powerful effect in creating confusion and some disbelief in an inquiring mind.

Certainly as a youth Sam Clemens was exposed to Calvinism, but he also encountered other strands of the whole Christian cloth. Wecter reports that Jane Clemens had young Sam attending the elementary class held in the shabby Old Ship of Zion Methodist Church where pupils memorized Bible verses and won the right to borrow from the library moralizing tales for good little boys. As he grew older, around ten or eleven when his mother and sister Pamela became Presbyterians, he was obliged to stay for the sermon and hear the Calvinist preaching on hellfire and the predestined elect that Tom Sawyer endured.[14] Sam Clemens himself remembered the Campbellite "crusade" that came to Hannibal first in the fall of 1845 and again in October-November 1852. In his autobiography he treats both as a single event to illustrate his own childhood innocence and wonder. No church in town, he noted, was big enough to accommodate all comers so the evangelist preached outdoors. The congregation was so large that it changed the boy's conception of the number of people on the face of the earth.[15] Sam Clemens also recalled the Millerite frenzy in Hannibal when localites who believed in William Miller's prediction that the world would end on October 22, 1844 dressed up in their "ascension robes" and gathered by the river's edge some two miles below Hannibal to see the Judgment Day dawn before their very eyes.[16] Still another thread of what Clemens later referred to as "wildcat" religion was evident in the Hannibal of his youth. "Spiritualism," said to have "convulsed" the town during the last three or four years Sam Clemens remained at home, began in 1849 and spread so rapidly that according to the Hannibal <u>Tri-Weekly Messenger</u> on December 23, 1852, "nearly every family has two or three mediums in it . . ." including families of Clemens's playmate Bill League and a schoolmate Betty Ruffner.[17] Twain's memories of "spiritualists" and village atheists are evident in his piece called "Villagers of 1840-43," which includes mention of a particularly violent case of insanity yoked to "religion," that of a young man chained and locked into a small house in the corner of a yard who "believed his left hand had committed a mortal sin." He chopped the hand off with a hatchet, escaped imprisonment, and chased his stepmother with a knife.[18]

These accounts of happenings in the Hannibal of his youth make evident that Twain was exposed to more than a simple Calvinistic Presbyterianism, which if dry and tendentious nevertheless stressed the doctrine of limited atonement. A less intellectually rigorous Christianity would have reached him through the Millerites prophesying the destruction of the earth, a Campbellite emotionalism stressing the lurid flames of hellfire, and a Spiritualism almost totally non-rational-all Christian. Such diverse Christian beliefs should have caused confusion in an intellectually active youngster like Sam Clemens. Had his parents been rigid in their beliefs, defended those beliefs against all comers, and passed those beliefs directly to the child, it is possible that the boy could have escaped doubt. But Jane Clemens herself was tolerant of all religions and other family members were farther from orthodoxy than were most of the community.

Of his father John Marshall Clemens's religious views, Sam Clemens said, "he attended no church and never spoke of religious matters, and had no part or lot in the pious joys of his Presbyterian family, nor ever seemed to suffer from this deprivation."[19] Wecter concluded of Sam's father that he was in his elder days held to be a "free-thinker or an agnostic."[20] Of his favorite uncle, John Quarles, Sam said, "I have never run across a better man than he was," and John Quarles was reportedly a Universalist, though there is no record to show that he was ever a member of a particular Universalist Church congregation.[21] It is not unlikely that Quarles's unconventional creed (embracing the belief in a kindly disposed Almighty who would save everybody) also encouraged the young Clemens's tendency toward an acceptance of Deism. Certainly when Clemens was a cub-printer and likely to be aware of any community event, he would have been aware of Hannibal's public debate over Universalism in 1851 between Elder Hopson, a Presbyterian, and an itinerant Universalist named Caples. Hopson expounded the system of salvation defending Calvinistic predestination; apparently Caples's response went unreported in the local press.[22] Again in 1852 Universalist was pitted against the orthodox in the public debate between a Rev. W. M. Rush and the Rev. E. Manford of St. Louis. According to the Hannibal Journal for July 15, 1852, Manford claimed that the Scriptures teach neither the doctrine of unconditional election, a final day of judgment, nor endless punishment of those "who die in disobedience to the Gospel," but the "final holiness and happiness of all mankind."[23]

Not only was Clemens exposed to non-Calvinist thought in his youth, but that he also rubbed elbows with an irreverence toward orthodox Christianity is apparent in an anecdote he tells about Wales McCormick, an associate printer on the Hannibal Courier. When the great revivalist Alexander Campbell came to Hannibal, some of his followers wanted a particular sermon of the revivalist printed. The cub-printers, Sam Clemens and Wales McCormick, working in the <u>Courier</u> printshop left two words out of the "book" when they printed it up. Their mistake was to cost them their Saturday afternoon off. Wales solved the problem by substituting the initials "J.C." into the line where the words "the name of Jesus Christ" were supposed to be. Campbell himself caught the error and again the cub-printers were in trouble when McCormick changed "J.C." into "Jesus H. Christ."[24] Young Sam Clemens's admiration for his co-worker's display of irreverence toward the great Alexander Campbell and a messing with a part of the sacred trinity suggests either that the elder Clemens's erring memory caused him to inject a mature judgment into this account or that by age seventeen one side of his religious nature was already inclining toward some scepticism on religious matters. Indeed, the notion of a fairly strong scepticism in a frontier Hannibal is strongly asserted by Minnie Brashear, who by no means approves of some of Twain's more irreverent skeptical writing. Brashear claimed that "professional men" in the Hannibal area were likely to be "free thinkers of the Jefferson type" though they would not have advertised their beliefs as such.[25]

DeVoto pointed to still another thread woven through the Hannibal religious fabric when he claimed that the living religion of the American negro slave for the young Clemens growing up in Hannibal was "the only religion that was ever vital to him."[26] DeVoto doubtless overstated the case, but he does show the evidence for the slaves' religion of terror influencing Twain, something clearly commented upon by Clemens himself in harking back to the stormy night after receiving the news of Injun Joe's death:

> By my teachings I perfectly well knew what all that wild rumpus was for--Satan had come to get Injun Joe. I had no doubt about it. It was the proper thing when a person like Injun Joe was required in the under world and I should have thought it strange and unaccountable if Satan had come for him in a less spectacular way. With every glare of lightning I shriveled and shrank together in mortal terror, and in the interval of black darkness that followed I poured out my lamentings over my lost condition, and my supplications for just one more chance, with an energy and feeling and sincerity quite foreign to my nature.[27]

Certainly this passage makes clear that young Sam Clemens was responsive to strong religious impressions. And one could argue that his conviction that Satan was coming for Injun Joe is evidence of a strong Calvinist influence derived from Presbyterianism through his church or his family. But it can also be argued that the emphasis on terror is a consequence of "wildcat" religion from the tents of the evangelists or from "spiritualists" or even the "living religion" of the slaves. In fact, all of these influences stress directly or indirectly hellfire and brimstone and active agents of evil working in the world--except perhaps for a staid Presbyterianism. What is not readily apparent here in this passage is a Universalist doctrine of salvation for all. If the elder Sam Clemens is accurate in his assessment of his own youth, however, careful attention needs to be paid to the last extended phrase in this passage--"energy and feeling and sincerity quite foreign to my nature." This phrase implies that some earlier "lamentings and supplications" were neither energetic, felt, nor sincere, and claims a "nature" quite at odds with such feelings, such energy, and such sincerity. Thus, there would be, at least in Clemens's mature mind the idea of a boy already partially at odds with doctrines and beliefs received from his environment, a boy by <u>nature</u> somewhat skeptical of revealed religion except in situations threatening hellfire. But in such situations, though they may not have been according to his "nature," his feelings, energy, and sincerity are real. This, in turn, suggests that finally Clemens was immune to so-called "reasoned" doctrines of churches or to those churches relying upon doctrine for an unimpassioned sermon to church members already saved and emotionally disengaged from their religion or totally cynical and hypocritical about it. And surely the young Clemens saw numerous such church members. On the other hand, the "wildcat" religion, the religion of slaves, no matter how non-rational, would have been a "felt" religion and its proponents sincere, no matter how unintellectual. The boy would have responded to the conviction if his own family scoffed.

So young Sam Clemens was subjected to more than a simple Calvinism stressing a pessimism that colored his final vision of God, universe, and man, and these separate religious influences would have had moral corollaries he would have absorbed, found contradictory, and would have needed to somehow resolve. As Kaplan pointed out in other ways, Clemens was a divided Mark

Twain-Mr. Clemens. One side of him knew; the other side hoped. Sometimes one voice was louder than the other, but both voices were always present. Though this division is evident from Clemens's earliest experiences to his last writings, it does not, as has been suggested, add up to a final negation of life, of the damned human race, of the universe, or of God. Rather it shows that, as a result of his apostasy from orthodox faith, something Sam Clemens gave up fairly early in his life, he was put in the modern position of finding an alternative. His life was a quest for that alternative. He could not accept what the established Church said. He could not completely rely upon his reason as the 18th century Rationalists did. He could not rely upon his feelings as early 19th century Romantics did for "intimations of immortality." He could not finally accept the scientific determinism his own age came to. He floundered through the options, confused, angry, pained at and in a secular world. This spiritual confusion, however, has an inherent consistency in keeping with someone spiritually alive, someone who persists in asking the big questions of the universe. Such conclusions emerge when, as subsequent discussion will demonstrate, one understands that Clemens merely followed chronologically the development of American religious thought up to and through his own time. It was finally not Clemens's fault that the thought of his nation and age was not ultimately sufficient to answer the big questions. The questions are still with us.

ENDNOTES TO CHAPTER I

1. "Mark Twain's Pessimistic Philosophy," Current Literature, Vol. 48, no. 6 (June 1910), 643-47 p. 643.
2. Albert Bigelow Paine, Mark Twain: A Biography (New York: Harper, 1912), three volumes, Vol. I, p. 39.
3. By my count Brooks refers to the biography 168 times. See William Wasserstrom, The Legacy of Van Wyck Brooks: A Study of Maladies and Motives (Carbondale and Edwardsville: Southern Illinois University Press, 1971), pp. 44-45.
4. Walter Sutton, Modern American Criticism (Englewood Cliffs, New Jersey: Prentice Hall, 1963), p. 14.
5. Bernard DeVoto Mark Twain's America (Boston: Little, Brown, 1932), p. 239.
6. Mark Twain's America, p. 239.
7. "The Mysterious Stranger: Mark Twain's Texts and the Paine-Duneka Edition," reprinted in Mark Twain's The Mysterious Stranger and the Critics, ed. John S. Tuckey (Belmont, California: Wadsworth Publishing Company, 1968), pp. 85-90.
8. Justin Kaplan, Mr. Clemens and Mark Twain (New York: Simon and Schuster, 1966), p. 80.
9. "Letters to the Book Review Editor," Saturday Review, XLIX (July 30, 1966), p. 28.
10. John T. Frederick, The Darkened Sky: Nineteenth Century

American Novelists and Their Religions (Notre Dame, Indiana: University of Notre Dame Press, 1969), p. 171.

11. Samuel Charles Webster, Ed., Mark Twain: Business Man (Boston: Little, Brown, 1946), p. 40.

12. Dixon Wecter, Sam Clemens of Hannibal (Boston: Houghton-Mifflin, 1952), p. 86.

13. Wecter, p. 228.

14. Wecter, p. 228.

15. Charles Neider, ed., The Autobiography of Mark Twain (New York: Harper, 1959), p. 90.

16. Wecter, p. 89.

17. Wecter, p. 90.

18. Walter Blair, ed., Mark Twain's Hannibal, Huck & Tom (Berkeley, California: University of California Press, 1969), pp. 37-38.

19. Following the Equator, II, 18, in The Writings of Mark Twain, Author's National Edition, 25 vols. (New York: Harper, 1907-1918), SVI, 18. Hereafter this edition is cited as Writings.

20. Wecter, p. 15.

22. Alexander E. Jones, "Heterodox Thought in Mark Twain's Hannibal," Arkansas Historical Review, X (Spring, 1951), 244-257 (pp. 245-46).

23. Alexander E. Jones, p. 252.

24. Neider, Autobiography, p. 91.

25. Minnie M. Brashear, Mark Twain Son of Missouri (Chapel Hill, North Carolina: University of North Carolina Press, 1934),

pp. 254-55.

26. DeVoto, <u>Mark Twain's America</u>, pp. 46, 37.
27. Neider, <u>Autobiography</u>, pp. 68 ff.

CHAPTER II: LEAVING HOME

From the view of the universe he held at his death in 1910, whether a despairing pessimism or something completely different, Samuel Clemens was a long way from Hannibal's boyhood influences of Calvinism, spiritualism, Universalism, slave religion, and even free thinking and agnosticism. But when he left Hannibal in June 1853 to find a job as a printer in St. Louis, he took with him Hannibal and its moral imperatives, its prejudices, its religious teachings and their consequences--heavy gear for life's journey, especially for an eighteen-year-old. He made it safely to St. Louis with everything intact, but it didn't take him long to unload the excess baggage for the rest of the trip.

Hannibal was indeed repressive and somewhat puritanical. Wecter notes that in the Spring of 1845 when Sam Clemens was nine, the city fathers banned the Sunday sale of liquor and the playing of billiards, nine pins, or "other games of amusement."[1] According to Paine, when young Sam prepared to leave home, his mother took up the Bible, placed his hand beside her own, and extracted from him the promise not to drink or play cards while he was away from home, a moral stricture in keeping with a rigid Presbyterianism.[2] And there is evidence that Sam began life away from home obeying his mother. At age 18, he writes criticizing easterners as "whiskey-swilling, God despising heathens" and believes himself to be the only one in his newspaper office that "does not drink."[3]

From the Protestant Crusade that swept through Hannibal in his boyhood and from Hannibal itself, Clemens absorbed obvious prejudices against all things "un-American." That the institution of slavery was sanctioned by his community and its churches, he himself pointed out:

> I was not aware that there was anything wrong with [slavery]. No one arraigned it in my hearing; the local papers said nothing against it; the local pulpits taught us that God approved it, that it was a holy thing and that the doubter need only look in the Bible if he wished to settle his mind.[4]

Although DeVoto rightly noted that the young Sam Clemens at some point learned from his father, John Marshall Clemens, that "slavery was a great wrong,"[5] even here the youth would have been confronted with conflicting moral imperatives from influence in his early life. Nevertheless, his Protestant Crusade prejudices were firmly entrenched. In a letter from Philadelphia in 1853, Sam Clemens comments on the presence of "many abominable foreigners . . . who hate everything American."[6] In a letter to his mother from New York he refers to "Niggers, mulattoes, quadroons, Chinese" as "human vermin."[7] And, of course, he would have picked up anti-Semitism from his same Hannibal sources. Another letter from this period refers to a home in Philadelphia that has been desecrated by being "occupied by a Jew."[8] The strongest evidence that Clemens's prejudices were the consequence of the Protestant Crusade effected primarily through the Presbyterian and Methodist churches and not simply random and occasional anti-Christian, anti-white subjects of ire lies in his prolonged distrust of Catholicism, dating back to Hannibal when Clemens's brother Orion (just after Sam left home) wrote in his <u>Daily Journal</u> that the Catholic Church was "equivalent to universal blight."[9] Sam Clemens shares these sentiments in a letter from St. Louis in 1855 when he writes Orion wishing "bad luck" to a new Catholic paper.[10]

In 1876 in a letter written to Frank E. Burrough, his St. Louis roommate in 1854-55, Sam Clemens described himself as he was at about the time he was making such bigoted statements: "Ignorance, intolerance, egotism, self-assertion, opaque perception, dense and pitiful chuckleheadedness--and almost pathetic unconsciousness of it all. That is what I was at 19 or 20."[11]

But if Clemens's prejudices go back to the Protestant Crusade in Hannibal, there is evidence of some disaffiliation from and criticism of churches as early as 1855 when he comments on a widow with five hungry children on her way from Arkansas to Illinois and destitute, cold, and tired in conjunction with "the handsome sum our preacher" gathered for "ignorant heathen in some far off part of the world."[12] Such an early critical tone strikes not at religious doctrine nor at Christianity, but at the organizational-institutional structure of the Church and at a myopia requiring different criteria for "us" than for "them," the same sort of myopia that he will level a few years later against the practice of missionarying. Implicit here too is not just the idea quoted in the same letter that the Bible instructs the disciples "to carry their good works into all the world--beginning first at Jerusalem," but that Americans perhaps should first look after their own. In fact, it is possible to see here a polarizing between loyalties to church and to nation. If this is the case, it is clear that Clemens is on the side of the nation. And if forced to a choice between the two and if Clemens chose the country, where would he be when he lost faith in America during the Gilded Age?

His prejudices and jingoism are evident in the Thomas Jefferson Snodgrass pieces written for a paper in Keokuk, Iowa.[13] The letters, so crude and vulgar that Clemens later denied their authorship, are filled with derogatory references to Germans, Irish and Jews.[14] But it is shortly after this that Clemens, by his account to A. B. Paine, is supposed to have read Thomas Paine's <u>The Age of Reason</u>, a book that could very well have been pivotal in his spiritual life. Minnie Brashear speculates that Clemens may have been familiar with Paine while he was still in Hannibal or perhaps in Philadelphia shortly after leaving home, but Clemens himself told A. B. Paine that he read <u>The Age of Reason</u> while a cub-pilot on the Mississippi, "read it with fear and hesitation, but marvelling at its fearlessness and wonderful power."[15] Thomas Paine's work, which attempts to establish the premises and the logical foundation for Deism, is in large part devoted to the irrationality and barbarity of much of Scripture. That Clemens read it with "fear and hesitation" is strong evidence of the triumph of orthodox Christianity in the Hannibal of his childhood; it is also evidence of his own attachment to orthodoxy until the time he read the work. His father, John Marshall Clemens, may well have been an agnostic, but his son was not of his persuasion if at that time he read The Age of Reason in "fear and hesitation". That the book was influential in shaping his thought is suggested by the fact that he remembers reading it some fifty years afterward and by his telling A. B. Paine at the time that he had just reread the book and "was amazed to see how tame it had become."[16] People do not ordinarily remember for fifty years later. Under any circumstances, if Clemens is telling the truth in saying he read The Age of Reason while a cub-pilot, he was at that point fully and completely introduced to heterodox thought.

    Still, in June 1858, he could yet echo his childhood faith in his conscience-stricken prayer as he watched his beloved brother Henry die in agony after the explosion of the steamboat Pennsylvania, blaming himself for hastening the end by giving Henry an excessive dose of a pain-killing drug:

> Oh, God! this is hard to bear. Hardened, hopeless, --aye, lost--lost and ruined sinner that I am--I, even I, have humbled myself to the ground and prayed as never man prayed before that the great God might let this cup pass from me--that he would pour out the fullness of his just wrath upon my wicked head, but have mercy, mercy, mercy upon that unoffending boy.[17]

Such rhetoric sounds quite "literary" and the emotion a little strained or vice versa, which need not deny to Sam Clemens either strong feeling or genuine guilt over his brother's death. On the other hand, it is possible that the emotion rings somewhat hollow because Clemens's faith has been damaged by a reading of Paine and that Clemens is striving for a consolation he needs from a source in which he does not believe. It is possible too that a good strong Puritan conscience could have made him believe his reading of Paine and his weakening of faith were sins punished through his brother's death. This may well have been a crucial time in the development of Clemens's religious outlook. Gladys Bellamy speculates that the death of Henry Clemens may well have started Sam Clemens asking "his lifelong question: Why?"[18]

A long-accepted error regarding the development in Clemens's religious view during his early years as a printer and immediately prior to his days as a cub-pilot is that he dramatically lost his orthodox faith and swallowed whole the philosophy of determinism and the concept of man as the lowest animal in creation. That conclusion resulted from speculation about Clemens's nightly conversations over a six-month period with a man named Macfarlane, a fellow lodger in Cincinnati in 1856-57. Originally set forth in Paine's authorized biography, the notion has been effectively destroyed by Paul Baender's demonstrating that for the deterministic influence of Macfarlane on Clemens, Paine used a single manuscript fragment written in 1897-98 as an autobiographical fragment rather than the fictional fragment that Twainians since Paine's biography in 1912 have considered it to be.[19] Again, if Clemens was correct in saying he read The Age of Reason "as a cub-pilot," he would not have read it in fear and hesitation if he had already departed from orthodoxy through Macfarlane's influence.

By 1860 Clemens's attitude toward religious orthodoxy is at least ambiguous. His niece, Annie Moffett, eight years old at the time, remembers telling her father she thought her twenty-four-year-old uncle Sam lacking in good sense because

> I told him the story of Moses and the bullrushes and he said he knew Moses very well; that he kept a second-hand store on Market Street. I tried very hard to explain that it wasn't the Moses I meant, but he just <u>couldn't</u> understand.[20]

Clemens, at this time, is certainly not above refusing to take seriously an old Bible story. In this same year, in a letter to his brother Orion, Sam Clemens remarks casually, "What a man wants with religion in these breadless times, surpasses my comprehension."[21] What he means by "religion" is not exactly clear in this and in other contexts in his later writings. Religion may well be a set of beliefs, acceptance of the trinity for instance; it may be a spirit as in the "religious spirit;" or it may be the institution of the church. Of these three possible meanings, Clemens's meaning here seems to be religious dogma or beliefs. It is not totally clear that he ever lost the emotional religious "feeling," though it is quite clear that the feeling eventually could not be evoked by the lore of the church. Again in 1860 Sam Clemens purportedly wrote to Orion, "I cannot see how a man of any large degree of humorous perception can ever be religious--except he purposely shut the eyes of his mind & keep them shut by force."[22] This statement clearly does not refer to institutional religion, but to a religious apprehension of the way things work in the world. It also implies that the emotions or feelings play no part in one's religious apprehension of the world. Here, then, is a clear reliance upon Reason to come to grips with reality and truth, a consequence perhaps of the reading of The Age of Reason a year or so earlier. Intellectually at this point Clemens seems to have cast off not only institutional religion, but the dogma of institutional Christianity, of which he may have been long suspicious.

Clemens's reliance upon reason does not divorce him completely from a Deistic interpretation of reality, except that Deism too must be regarded as a "religion," and Clemens says he has no use for it and finds it intellectually unacceptable. If this is true, then his association with Freemasonry in the early 1860's must be explained on other grounds such as Freemasonry's close ties to Deism. Evidence exists to show that while Clemens was still a pilot his membership petition was presented on December 26, 1860, to the Polar Star Lodge Number Seventy-Nine, and was favorably reported on by February 13, 1861. Clemens rose rapidly in the lodge and became a Master Mason by July 10 of the same year, just sixteen days before he headed for the Nevada Territory. Alexander E. Jones contends that there are several parallels between Clemens's fundamental thinking on religion and Albert Pike's (Pike was the most distinguished Masonic writer of the period) and "more than a hundred passages" in Clemens's writings similar to "basic teachings" of Freemasonry, that indeed Freemasonry introduced Twain to "a specialized type of deism."[23]

Evidence from Clemens's stay in the Far West substantiates a declining interest in institutionalized religion and an increasing concern with the morality of a secular world, an attitude in keeping with Deism, Masonry, or freethinking. In a letter to his mother form Carson City, Nevada dated October 26, 1861, Clemens answers questions put him by his mother:

> "First--do I go to church on Sunday?" Answer--"Scasely." Second--"Have you a church in Carson?" We have--a Catholic one--but, to use a fireman's expression, I believe "they don't run her now." We have also Protestant service every Sabbath in the schoolhouse. Third--"Are there many ladies in Carson?" Multitudes--probably the handsomest in the world. Fourth--"Are the citizens generally moral and religious?" Prodigiously so.[24]

As I construe this, Clemens has used a heavy irony in his response to his mother. By "scasely," he means "if ever." That "they don't run her now," shows the irrelevance of the church in general, and his only "believing" the church is not in operation shows his own indifference to whether it is or not. The "handsomest ladies in the world" at the mining camp in Nevada must mean flamboyantly dressed and made up prostitutes. And the only way the citizenry in such a setting could be regarded as "prodigiously" moral and religious is by adhering to the word rather than the deed in "moral and religious." This may be overstating the irony, but it certainly seems probable. But whether Clemens was uninterested in religion at the time or his new environment made religion something to not write about, he saw enough of mankind and its ways in Nevada, especially as a political reporter covering frontier democracy in action, to show an unmistakable bent for moral reform. Here too he could have been influenced by Thomas Paine's line, "My religion is to do good."

One of Twain's stories from the time, a hoax called "The Dutch Nick Massacre," seems aimed mainly at the San Francisco Water Company's stockrigging which had financially ruined innocent stockholders.[25] Yet another piece written in Clemens's lengthy coverage during 1863-64 of the final session of the Nevada Territory's Constitutional attacks on Bill Stewart, whom Clemens saw as "construing" the Constitution to achieve his own selfish ends. These pieces provide evidence of Clemens's growing awareness of the evil in the world, an implied inadequacy of the church to do anything about evil, the indifference of the church to evil, and the cloaking of evil in the garb of religion. As Clemens says of Stewart, "Give him a chance to construe the sacred law, and there wouldn't be a damned soul in perdition in a month."[26] Stewart then will erase the meaning of evil. Such a stance earned Clemens the description of "moral phenomenon." If Sam Clemens is following a deistic bent at this point in his life, his concern with evil as an active force in the world is certainly not rationalistic.

When Clemens moved from Nevada to California, he wrote that he had decided to commit himself to writing "to excite the laughter of God's creatures."[27] In such a commitment, he implicitly accepts the notion of a caring God. At the same time, he admits to his brother Orion that his two earliest ambitions as a boy are behind him--being a preacher and a riverboat pilot; he cannot be a preacher, he says, because he lacked "the necessary stock in trade--i.e., religion."[28] So Clemens is in the position of lacking religion, yet committing himself to writing for "God's creatures." Religion then must be institutionalized orthodox Christianity in this context. It is worth noting that Clemens mentioned his childhood ambition of preaching to A. B. Paine as deriving from his conviction that it "looked like a safe job," since a preacher ran no risk of being damned.[29] This Calvinistic fear of hell so strong in his youth could have been some of the stock in trade he lacked by the time he had gone to California.

In California, Clemens continued in the spirit of reform begun in Nevada. He again attacked government officials, the San Francisco police for inefficiency and neglect of duty, the coroner and his employees for being arrogant and unresponsive to their masters, the people.[30] For the first time he is overtly critical of the clergy and posed as having offered three prominent Eastern ministers a chance for a "call" in San Francisco with each turning him down because he was making more money in his home pastorate investing in cotton, petroleum, or grain markets.[31] Such criticism simply reinforces what should be apparent at this time in Clemens's life: he is not sympathetic to institutionalized religion and he is morally offended by people professing spiritual concern and devoting their energies to materialism.

Clemens's argument against institutionalized or organized

religion takes several forms. He attacks indirectly the church's refusal to be realistic or its insistence on offering overly simplistic solutions to problems. Thus he writes "The Story of a Bad Little Boy that Bore a Charmed Life" about the sinner James, who stole, lied, and yet came to wealth, all in sharp contrast to what happened to the sinful little Jameses of story books.[32] The point seems clear. The moral laws taught to children are not the path to the success advocated by those who taught the moral laws. Thus there are, as Emerson pointed out, two laws--one for man and one for things. The church must make up its mind and decide which side it is on: it must teach virtue, but it must not stupidly advise that virtue is easy, a point made explicit in the later story "The Man Who Corrupted Hadleyburg." A companion piece to "The Story of a Bad Little Boy," titled "The Story of a Good Little Boy Who Did Not Prosper" and published five years later in the Galaxy, tells of a paragon of virtue named Jacob Blivens who "always obeyed his parents" regardless of the ridiculousness of their demands and was "so honest that he was simply ridiculous." All of Jacob's goodness and honesty and ambition to make a dying speech proclaiming the moral wisdom in Sunday school books is inadequate to keep him from being scattered by nitroglycerin over so many townships that "they had to hold five inquests on him to find out whether he was dead or not."[33] Twain had begun his campaign against unrealistic Sunday school literature in a Nevada piece entitled "Stories for Good Little Boys and Girls," which ridiculed the success-at-any-price formula.³⁴ He was not being particularly courageous in attacking the literature in California, however, because he had heard the Presbyterian minister Dr. Wadsworth himself attack such books in San Francisco.³⁵

It is possible to see Twain's attack on such Sunday school yarns as ridicule of childhood ideas of "Compensation and inevitable retribution here on earth," and implicit encouragement of the idea that this is "an amoral universe," as Branch has suggested.³⁶ Clemens certainly ridicules the easy childhood formulas of virtue rewarded, and clearly implies that scoundrelism pays in this world. But this does not mean the universe is amoral. There is no inconsistency between such attacks and Clemens's statement that his new calling is to provide laughter for "God's creature."

Clemens shows at this time another side of his complex upbringing in poking fun at the hollowness of Presbyterianism's hell-fire-and-brimstone creed and its meaningless ritual when he defends "wildcat" religion. To the extremely fervent Spiritualists in San Francisco, he brags of "us cool Presbyterians," who "get up of a Sunday morning and put on the best harness we have got and trip cheerfully down town;" subside "into solemnity and enter the church;" stand up and "duck our heads and bear down on a hymn book propped on the pew in front when the minister prays;" stand up again while the "hired" choir sings; look "in the hymn book and check off the verses to see that they don't shirk any of the stanzas;" sit "silent and grave" during the preaching; and "count the waterfalls and bonnets furtively, and catch flies;" grab their "hats and bonnets when the benediction is begun;" and when "it is finished," rush out; . . . You never see any of us Presbyterians getting in a sweat about religion."[37] What Twain is reacting to here precisely, and it is reaction against not advocacy for, is the "cool" with which he begins. He does not like the absence of emotion and the lack of intensity, which add up to a lack of conviction. Such church members "put on" and "subside into" their religion, which precludes its being integral with them. The music and song are "hired," not a consequence of feeling, and, of course, they check to see that they get their money's worth by checking off the verses the choir sings. For those who are "cool" in their religion, there is indeed no "sweat." If spiritualists are ignorant or naive, they at least are willing to act upon a belief that is felt. With impish irony, Twain is holding up this Presbyterian service as a model for the Spiritualists accused by local self-righteous and complacent churchgoers of driving converts insane with the fervor accompanying conversion. As Bellamy points out, Clemens had seen Methodist camp meetings and Campbellite revivals which had "earlier stocked the asylums with lunatics, and nobody said a word," but now the public is concerned because the religion is "wildcat," a new unaccustomed breed.[38] In the same mocking tone, he boasts of the Presbyterian hereafter, with its clear-out division between saints and sinners and their sharply contrasting rewards, particularly its superiority to the heterodox "wildcat" religion's hereafter and its vague, new-fangled, deist-like uncertainty and endless struggle for perfection. Since he can speak with first-hand knowledge, Twain poses as a "brevet" member of Dr. Wadsworth's congregation, one who has been "sprinkled in infancy," so that he claims "the right to be punished as a Presbyterian" in the hereafter," . . . the substantial Presbyterian . . . fire and brimstone" rather than the wildcat "heterodox hell of remorse of conscience," which, he says, is "vague and ill-defined." The Presbyterian hell is total "misery"; its heaven complete happiness with "nothing to do." "But when a man dies on a wildcat basis, he will never rightly know"; wildcat's heaven, unlike the Presbyterian's with "nothing to do" is devoted to "pro-gress, pro-gress-study, study, study . . . and if that isn't hell I don't know what is," and in the wildcat's "bad place he will be worried by remorse of conscience." [39] The choice Twain presents here is no choice at all for someone who no longer accepts established Christian doctrine through the Scriptures, the very basis of Presbyterian belief in both heaven and hell. In the absence of some authority such as Scripture or church, such a person is put in the position of finding his own source of faith, the very position described humorously by Twain as not knowing "which department he is in." The dispute is over something Clemens probably was not very concerned with at the time, an afterlife, but what seems to lie at the basis of the distinction he is drawing between "wildcat" and "Presbyterian" is that of epistemology. These knowing Presbyterians who have easily divided an afterlife into a heaven (where there is nothing to do) and a hell (where all is misery) are to be bothered not at all by the tough questions, the "study" required to know something or the "remorse of conscience" which is a hell on earth and therefore rather secular.

When Spiritualism created a stir in San Francisco and especially when the local *Bulletin* reported several cases of insanity resulting from "undue exposure" to Spiritualism, Clemens investigated the group's activities, even going so far as to ask questions of seance leaders and later at one seance to sit on the stage as a member of a committee to umpire the proceedings.[40] He concluded simply that ". . . it is mighty hard to believe what you don't know,"[41] yet he treated the seances with what Branch has called "tempered respect" while leaving the impression the seances were "relatively harmless frauds."[42] Twain pokes fun at the Spiritualists, but he is harder finally on the Presbyterians; their ideas of heaven and hell--in the absence of evidence-- would also be "vague and ill-defined."

Finally, Clemens's religious development in San Francisco is perhaps best revealed by two sketches he wrote early in 1866: "Sabbath Reflections" and "Reflections on the Sabbath."[43] The first sketch is a brief dramatic monologue that reveals the narrator thinking out loud about an ideal Sabbath. The lofty ideality of his reflection upon a day "set apart by a benignant Creator" for repose and meditation upon eternity is destroyed by the grating reality of successive distraction: Brown's howling dog that Brown persists in keeping penned up, the hoarse-voiced rooster's crowing, the cackling hen, the cat fight. As Henry Nash Smith pointed out, Twain here presents two contrasting visions of the universe--a world of nature and fact opposed to a world of ideality and spirit.[44] There should be no question about which of the two worlds is real. Twain's ridicule and criticism of most institutions and people seem to constantly go back to the failure of the institution or the individual to face reality or truth and the insistence upon hiding truth or reality behind some religious sham or political verbiage passing for uprightness.

The second sketch, "Reflections on the Sabbath," pretends to back off from criticizing "the wisdom of the Creator," but proceeds to do just that--to question and to meddle in His "exclusive affairs." As Branch points out, "the piece is prophetic" in that Twain would continue to employ reason to explain "man's origin, nature, and destiny" throughout his career.[45]

By the time Sam Clemens left California for the Sandwich Islands, he had been exposed to a variety of religious belief and seems, at that time, to be on the side of a secular religion of reason. He had left behind the trappings of Calvinist dogma and other unreasoning religious sects. He had not abandoned belief in a Creator and seems to have equated that Creator with natural laws that include barking dogs and fighting cats. Whatever he believed, it was not what he had been taught in the Sunday schools. He had seen much of the world and it did not square with most orthodox religious doctrine.

Twain's twenty-five reports from the Sandwich Islands when he served there as a roving correspondent for the Sacramento Union from March to August 1866 seem to mark a departure from convictions apparent in San Francisco. His assignment was to report back to California businessmen, and there is some evidence that Clemens simply hired his pen to these California moneyed interests. For instance, in San Francisco his sympathies seemed to be awakened to the plight of the Chinese. It is an old story how he, along with other San Franciscans, was at first guilty of cruel discrimination against Chinese immigrants--he and his crony Steve Gillis lived next to their shanty "tin-can houses" and created disturbances at night by throwing empty beer bottles on the tinny roofs.[46] But the Call editor suppressed Twain's news item detailing how butchers set their dogs on an offending Chinese youth while a policeman looked on amused. Clemens bided his time until 1870 when he published in Galaxy Magazine "Disgraceful Persecution of a Boy," criticizing the police, city bosses, and the California legislature for making a mockery of America's heritage as "an asylum for the poor and oppressed of all nations" by their collective cruelty to a Chinese when " a white man needed a scapegoat."

> Nobody loved Chinamen, nobody befriended them, nobody spared them suffering when it was convenient to inflict it; everybody, individuals, communities, the majesty of the state itself, joined in hating, abusing and

persecuting these humble strangers.[47]

Whether or not Clemens had by 1870 overcome so much of the racial bigotry evident in such early pieces as the "Snodgrass" letters or even that he had compassion for the Chinese while still living in San Francisco, he identified himself closely enough with the West Coast business community to advocate to Californians the use of Chinese coolies: "You will not always go on paying $80 and $100 a month for labor which you can hire for $5. The sooner California adopts coolie labor the better it will be for her."[48]

Clemens seems to have embraced some doctrine of progress and fallen back on some conventional concepts of the old Sunday school days when he writes of the natives' relationship to the United States. His republican, anti-aristocratic, pro-American eagle virtually shrieks in a defense of America's political and religious "liberators" of the oppressed natives, the Kanakas:

> The king and the chiefs ruled the common herd with a rod of iron; made them gather all the provisions the masters needed; . . . take kicks and cuffs for thanks; drag out their lives well flavored with misery, and then suffer death for trifling offenses or yield up their lives on sacrificial altars to purchase favors from the gods for their hard rulers.[49]

He is led to a defense of American influence in the islands, perhaps by the charge of the British clergyman Staley who Twain sees as claiming the natives are "morally and religiously in a worse condition than they were before the American missionaries ever came here." Twain asserts:

> Now that is not true--and in that respect the statement bears a strong family likeness to another of the bishop's remarks about our missionaries. Our missionaries are our missionaries--and even if they

> were our devils, I would not want any English prelate to slander them.[50]

Clearly Twain is led to his defense not because missionaries are sound Christian influences, but because they are Americans under attack by foreigners. Twain can be rhapsodic about the influence of the established church upon Hawaii; he writes of the ship steaming into Honolulu

> . . . to the music of six different church bells, which sent their mellow tones far and wide, over hills and valleys, which were peopled by naked, savage, thundering barbarians only fifty years ago! Six Christian churches within five miles of the ruins of a pagan temple, where human sacrifices offered up to hideous idols in the last century! . . . and lo! . . . descendants [of the savages] were at church! Behold what the missionaries have wrought![51]

If Clemens is not simply hiring his pen to commercial exploiters, it seems clear that he does not find it preferable to be a pagan suckled in a creed outworn. He is on the side of "civilization" as opposed to barbarians and of the Church as serving to bring these people into civilization. America, of course, represents the ultimate in civilization; therefore it is only right that Hawaiian agriculture, commerce, and mercantile affairs are in "the hands of Americans--republicans; the whole people are saturated with the spirit of democratic Puritanism, and they are --republicans. This is a republic, the very marrow, and over it sit a king, a dozen nobles, and half a dozen Ministers."[52] The missionaries who have brought this civilization are the "devoted old Puritan knights who have seen forty years of missionary service" and "that Puritan spirit which subdued America and underlies her whole religious fabric today--which has subdued these islanders . . ." is worthy of overt praise.[53]

Other evidence from Clemens's writing at the time suggests that he must have seen himself in the role of a propagandist committed to defending American interests against foreign influence no matter what the cost, because clearly he was not as one-sided in viewing the missionaries as the correspondence makes him out to be. He lists what seem to him to be the missionaries' chief virtues: "pious; hardworking; hard-praying; self-sacrificing, hospitable; devoted to the well-being of this people and the interests of Protestantism." Their less desirable traits--"bigoted; puritanical; slow; ignorant of all white human nature and natural ways of man . . . ; old fogy--fifty years behind the age; uncharitable toward the weaknesses of the flesh; considering all short-comings, faults, and failings in the light of crimes, and having no mercy and no forgiveness for such."[54] Here be it noted the term "puritanical" is not a virtue, yet Twain uses it in a positive sense to describe the American "spirit." When national pride is not directly involved, Twain laughs at the missionaries as purveyors of the Calvinist nonsense about heaven and hell he had grown up believing:

> . . . the missionaries braved a thousand privations to come and make [the natives] permanently miserable by telling them how beautiful and blissful a place heaven is, and how nearly impossible it is to get there; and showed the poor native how dreary a place perdition is and what unnecessarily liberal facilities there are for going to it.[55]

Evidently it is better to be a pagan than to be "permanently miserable." In the privacy of his notebook at the time, Clemens flippantly comments, "More missionaries and more row made over these 60,000 people than would take to convert hell."[56] Yet he himself has added to the "row," put in his oar to keep it going. Objectively, Clemens probably found it difficult to reconcile the missionaries' bringing barbarians into civilization with their propounding, implicitly or otherwise, a permanent misery; he was doubtlessly motivated by a strong patriotism and by those who hired him.

At this point in his career, in hiring out his pen, Sam Clemens inclined either to cynicism or patriotism. Though he attacked corruption in the city government in California and that in the State or Territorial government in Nevada, his faith in the United State obviously remained firm. Likewise, though he had attacked corruption in the San Francisco Water Company, he hired on to represent business in the Sandwich Islands. He is clearly on the side of civilization and progress, of education, industry, thrift, and all the other virtues of the 18th century rationalists. And reason is his tool for knowing, except when love of country is an issue. He is perturbed at the failure of the Church to be reasonable in espousing its moral demands, demands that are in conflict with what Clemens sees to be "natural," and he is overtly hostile to the Church's simplistic notions of heaven and hell. He is, at this point in his career, a rationalist getting by in the world, having left the simple Calvinism of his youth and not yet having accepted a romantic attitude or a later deterministic view of the universe.

ENDNOTES TO CHAPTER II

1. Wecter, p. 85.
2. Wecter, p. 262.
3. Webster, p. 18.
4. Neider, *Autobiography*, p. 6.
5. DeVoto, *Mark Twain's America*, p. 65.
6. *Letters*, I., p. 29.
7. Brashear, *Mark Twain: Son of Missouri*, pp. 156-57.
8. *Mark Twain's Letters to the Muscatine Journal*, ed. Edgar M. Branch (Chicago: The Mark Twain Association of America, 1942), see Branch's introduction, pp. 5-11.
9. Edgar M. Branch, *The Literary Apprenticeship of Mark Twain* (New York: Russell and Russell, 1966), p. 37.
10. *Letters to the Muscatine Journal*, p. 24.
11. *Letters to the Muscatine Journal*, p. 7. See *Letters*, I, p. 289.
12. *Letters to the Muscatine Journal*, p. 23.
13. Branch, *Apprenticeship*, p. 42.
14. Charles Hance, ed., *The Adventures of Thomas Jefferson Snodgrass* (Chicago: Pascal Covici, 1928).
15. Brashear, *Son of Missouri*, pp. 162, 163, 245.
16. Paine, III, p. 1445.
17. *Letters*, I, p. 40.
18. Gladys Bellamy, *Mark Twain as a Literary Artist* (Norman, Okla.: University of Oklahoma Press, 1950), pp. 75.

19. Paul Baender, "Alias Macfarlane: A Revision of Mark Twain's Biography," American Literature, Vol. 38, No. 2 (May 1966), pp. 187-97.
20. Webster, p. 39.
21. Letters, I, p. 45.
22. Phillip Foner, Mark Twain: Social Critic, (New York: International Publishers, 1958), p. 132; Foner does not cite his specific source for this quotation.
23. Alexander E. Jones, "Mark Twain and Freemasonry," American Literature, Vol. 26 (Nov. 1954), pp. 363-73.
24. Fred W. Lorch, "Mark Twain in Iowa," Iowa Journal of History and Politics, 29 (July 1929), pp. 408-56 (453ff.).
25. Published in the Enterprise on October 28, 1863; see Mark Twain of the Enterprise, eds. Henry Nash Smith and Frederick Anderson (Berkeley, California: University of California Press, 1957) p. 86.
26. Mark Twain of the Enterprise, p. 97.
27. Kaplan, Mr. Clemens and Mark Twain, p. 14.
28. Kaplan, p. 14.
29. Paine, I, 84.
30. Bernard Taper, Mark Twain's San Francisco (New York: McGraw Hill, 1963), pp. 51-53.
31. Paul A. Carter, The Spiritual Crisis of the Gilded Age (Dekalb, Ill.: Northern Illinois University Press, 1971), p. 186.
32. The Californian, December 23, 1865; reprinted by the

<u>Californian</u> December 22, 1866 under the title "The Story of the Bad Little Boy Who Bore a Charmed Life."

33. <u>Contributions to the Galaxy</u>, 1868-1871, by Mark Twain, ed. Bruce R. McElderry, Jr. (Gainesville, Florida: Scholars' Facsimiles and Reprints, 1961), pp. 44-46 (p. 44).

34. <u>Golden Era</u>, May 15, 1864. Merle Johnson's <u>Bibliography to the Works of Mark Twain</u> erroneously gives the publication date as May 15, 1863, exactly a year early.

35. "Reflections on the Sabbath," <u>The Washoe Giant in San Francisco</u>, by Mark Twain, Franklin Walker, ed. (San Francisco: George Fields, 1938), pp. 115-16.

36. Branch, <u>Apprenticeship</u>, p. 150.

37. "The New Wildcat Religion," <u>The Washoe Giant</u>, pp. 133-34.

38. Bellamy, <u>Mark Twain as a Literary Artist</u>, pp. 106-07.

39. "Reflections on the Sabbath," <u>The Washoe Giant</u>, pp. 115-16.

40. <u>The Washoe Giant</u>, p. 120.

41. Taper, <u>Mark Twain's San Francisco</u>, p. 215.

42. Branch, <u>Apprenticeship</u>, p. 145.

43. Taper, <u>Mark Twain's San Francisco</u>, pp. 199-200, 235-37.

44. Henry Nash Smith, <u>Mark Twain: The Development of a Writer</u> (Cambridge: Harvard University Press, 1962), pp. 4-5.

45. Branch, <u>Apprenticeship</u>, p. 147.

46. Mark Twain, <u>Sketches, New and Old</u>, V. 7, p. 129.

47. Mark Twain, <u>Sketches</u>, V. 7, p. 129.

48. <u>Mark Twain's Letters from Hawaii</u>, ed. by A. Grove Day (New York: Appleton Century, 1966), pp. vii, 93, 271; see

Mark Twain's Development as a Writer, p. 15.

49. *Letters from Hawaii*, p. 54.
50. *Letters from Hawaii*, p. 130.
51. *Letters from Hawaii*, p. 26.
52. *Letters from Hawaii*, p. 171.
53. *Letters from Hawaii*, pp. 172-73.
54. *Letters from Hawaii*, p. 129.
55. *Letters from Hawaii*, p. 53.
56. *Mark Twain's Notebook*, p. 21.

CHAPTER III: THE NEW PILGRIM'S PROGRESS

There is nothing particularly appealing in the Mark Twain of the Sandwich Islands--a clever, witty writer of no firm conviction, of considerable cynicism, and with only an unthinking patriotism and his reason to sustain him. Perhaps he was dissatisfied himself with what he had become, a hired pen, a scoffer at believers who were not really that dangerous to begin with, a mere promoter, like every other unthinking American, of the greatest country in the world. Perhaps after he returned from the Sandwich Islands and through his jumping frog leaped to the Eastern seaboard, Samuel Clemens felt some twinges of childhood Calvinistic guilt over his new literary prosperity. Whether he was in quest of some faith lost in childhood or whether he was simply a journalist looking for a story, for some reason Clemens booked himself aboard the Quaker City for an excursion to Europe and the Holy Land from June 8 to November 19, 1867 with a passenger list made up primarily of ministers and the utterly devout. Certainly Clemens's Quaker City trip and his courtship of Olivia Langdon up to his engagement to her in 1869 were events in a time of his seriously reconnoitering his old time religion.

From his excursion came The Innocents Abroad in which, as Kenneth S. Lynn says, the newborn, immature American "prepared to take over the age and [to] judge all the nations of the earth by his own."[1] In Clemens's judging lies the evidence for his somewhat unsteady religious stance at that time. Before the ship ever gets to Europe, Twain reveals strong anti-Catholic prejudices. At the Azores island of Fayal, a Portuguese agriculture colony, he damns the islanders for possessing "Portuguese characteristics." They are "slow, poor, shifty, sleepy, and lazy."[2] Evident here is a belief in national characteristics, perhaps inborn, perhaps acquired. Catholicism is obviously a part of the problem, as Twain indicates in citing a "good Catholic Portuguese" who "crossed himself and prayed God to shield him from all blasphemous desire to know more than his father before him."[3] Twain equates the desire for knowledge--in itself a positive characteristic--and a doctrine of progress implicit in the desire to know more than one's father with blasphemy in the eyes of the Church. The Church itself is actively deceptive; Twain writes that "It is in communities like this that Jesuit humbuggery flourishes."[4] And the consequence is gullibility and ignorance in the people, evident in Twain's mentioning the presence in the church of a piece of the cross on which Christ was crucified being extremely well preserved and yet "those confiding people believe in that piece of wood unhesitatingly."[5]

The negatives in such passages imply acceptance of some positive values. Clemens clearly believes in progress, in the capacity to know more than one's father, in knowledge, in honesty, reason--all of which he sees buried or prohibited by the

Catholic Church in cooperation with the "Portuguese" government or national character.

Clemens's Protestant indignation becomes even more pronounced when the excursionists reach Italy:

> We were in the heart and home of priestcraft--of a happy, cheerful, contented ignorance, superstition, degradation, poverty, indolence, and everlasting unaspiring worthlessness. And we said fervently, it suits these people precisely; let them enjoy it, along with the other animals . . .[6]

Such condemnation is not just that of Catholic by Protestant, but that of the 18th century rationalist. The antonyms of the condemning nouns are "knowledge, enlightenment, elevation, affluence, industry, and everlasting aspiring worth," almost a catalogue of Enlightenment aspirations of beliefs. The equation of "these people" with "the other animals" seems to imply that their condition is in part a matter of choice and that there is no "natural" virtue in them or in mankind. Man comes to be what he is through the exercise of his rational faculties to achieve "civilization."

Italy as a nation is condemned; for "fifteen hundred years, [she] has turned all her energies . . . to the building up a vast array of wonderful church edifices, and starving half her citizens to accomplish it."[7] Once more Twain yokes together church and state, finding both responsible for an inhumane consequence. And that Twain condemns an implicit tradition--fifteen hundred years--is as clear as the fact that he condemns the present Italy. His yardstick for measurement is the New World:

> All the churches in an ordinary American city put together could hardly buy the jewelled frippery in one of her cathedrals. And for every beggar in America, Italy can show a hundred--and rags and vermin to match. It is the wretchedest, princeliest land on earth.[8]

America as nation has escaped the rule of a church and evidently it is the church which is seen as the final oppressor when Twain exclaims, "'Oh, sons of classic Italy, *is* the spirit of enterprise, of self-reliance, of noble endeavor, utterly dead within ye? Curse your indolent worthlessness, why don't you rob your church?'"[9] The rhetoric suggests that the fault lies in the will of the people, that the nation may redeem itself through its people if it will deny its church.

Twain feels no reluctance in equating a degenerate morality with the Old World dominated by the priest. He grows livid in retelling the famous Abelard and Heloise love story, referring to Abelard as a "coldhearted villain . . . with the deliberate intention of debauching a confiding, innocent girl," who compounds his villainy by offering to marry Heloise on the "shameful condition . . . that the marriage be kept secret from the world, to the end that (while her good name remained a wreck, as before) his priestly reputation might be kept untarnished."[10]

Twain seems to thoroughly reject the Church-dominated old world in refusing to see progress from a Roman civilization to a Christianized Rome. He points out the barbarism of the Romans in turning the lions in on the Christians and immediately follows with the historical consequence of Christian victory over paganism:

when the Holy Mother Church became mistress of the
barbarians, she taught them the error of their ways by
no such means. No, they put them in this pleasant
Inquisition and pointed to the Blessed Redeemer, who
was also gentle and so merciful toward all men, and
they urged the barbarians to love him; and they did all
they could to persuade them to love and honor him--
first by twisting their thumbs out of joint with a
screw; then by nipping their flesh with pincers--red
hot ones, . . . then by skinning them alive a little,
and finally by roasting them in public. They always
convinced these barbarians. The true religion,
properly administered, as the good Mother Church used
to administer it, is very, very soothing . . .
wonderfully persuasive also.[11]

It is easy and legitimate to infer from this that the barbarians were less cruel than the "Holy Mother Church"; thus the Church has not advanced civilization but retarded it in some important ways. Twain goes beyond the Church itself in the last line of this passage by referring to "the true religion" which seems to mean Christianity and by implying perhaps that it is wonderfully "persuasive" when and only when it is so administered. Twain ironically concludes the section by summing up the difference between pagan and Christian: "One is the system of the degraded barbarians, the other of enlightened, civilized people."[12]

Whatever the evidence available to Clemens's eyes at the time, it is evident from his past that he had a strong bias against Catholicism before he ever saw a church in Rome. He may have abandoned his fundamentalist Calvinism before now, but he has not lost his Protestant suspicion of Catholicism or his American distrust of Europe.

But if Sam Clemens found the American Presbyterian's Europe, when the Quaker City sailed on to the Holy Land, he failed to find the "Presbyterian's Palestine"; as Allison Ensor suggests, he found instead a "skeptic's Palestine."[13] This is not to suggest that Clemens was not a skeptic on points of Scripture before he went to the Holy Land, but that his skepticism intensified.

Clemens has expressed in numerous places an active skepticism on religious matters up to the time of his arrival in the Hold Land. He may have read <u>The Age of Reason</u> "in fear and hesitation," but he also marvelled at its "fearlessness." He had expressed himself to Orion as not understanding the need for religion in "breadless times." But though he may well have adopted the attitudes of Deists or Masons and, like many 18th century thinkers, did not find "revelation" in Scripture, there was no reason for him to have questioned the overall historicity of Scripture. After all, "progressive" religions equated the piety of Jesus with that of Socrates. And there would have been for Clemens and for others a power and a nobility in the history from which the "revelation" had been wrung. His visit to the Holy Land destroyed the power and nobility and should have left Clemens even less secure than before in his convictions. Because though Clemens up to this time has attacked "Church" and "religion" and "missionaries," there is nothing to indicate that he is immune to a religious spirit, a spirit that could have been easily in keeping with Christ's teachings, that could prevail even when the "spirit" had been destroyed through the institution of the Church itself. But the physical presence of the Holy Land forced Sam Clemens to question the meaning of the history he had perhaps accepted as true. The dismal reality was in shocking contrast to the opulence and color of the Holy Land he had grown up believing in.

He was dumbfounded at differences between reality and his preconceptions. He says of the "sacred sea of Galilee" and of the Dead Sea, "when I was in Sunday school I thought they were sixty thousand miles in diameter."[14] The Sea of Galilee, only two thirds as large as the uncelebrated Lake Tahoe, was so narrow in fact, that when a boatman asked four dollars to ferry him across, Clemens is said to have remarked, "No wonder the Lord walked."[15] And the whole of Palestine was so small that

> leaving out two or three short journeys of the Savior, he spent his life, preached his gospel, and performed his miracles within a compass no larger than an ordinary county in the United States.[16]

And Twain is forced to realize, he said, that "I must studiously and faithfully unlearn a great many things I have somehow absorbed concerning Palestine."[17] Exactly how much "unlearning" took place is impossible to know, but Twain seems to become even more irreverent than he has been in the past. He quite rightly blames travel books for many of his mistaken notions, yet the gullibility of biblical commentators puts a strain on his early reverence and he comes down hard on the kind of scribbler who in "treating a scriptural subject [can] rave like a very lunatic, and yet escape criticism" and cites " the far-fetched conclusions of . . . curious prophecy-fulfillers" about Smyrna. The Scriptures implied that Smyrna would receive a "crown of life"--

if she proved to be "faithful unto death." To the prophecy-fulfillers Smyrna does now wear a crown of life. The fact is, Twain adds, she has had "a chequered career" for eighteen centuries under "the rule of princes of many creeds," and has been "utterly destroyed six times."[18]

Twain's impatience with his pious fellow excursionists who are rapturous over the "limited desolation" of Palestine is tempered by his understanding that "These men had been taught from infancy to revere, almost to worship, the holy places whereon their happy eyes were resting now." Nevertheless, it is Twain the empiricist, Twain the rationalist, who refuses to give up his sensory data and find Palestine anything other than "first in dismal scenery."[19] His impatience is revealed when three of his fellows believe so strictly in keeping the Sabbath holy that they refuse to travel on Sunday and thereby force a three day journey into two grueling days of travel:

> Nothing could move the pilgrims. They must press on. Men might die, horses might die, but they must enter upon holy soil next week, with no Sabbath-breaking stain upon them. They were willing to commit a sin against the spirit of religious law, in order that they might preserve the letter of it.[20]

If Twain is hard on his fellow excursionists' irrational religious zeal, he is brutal in his treatment of the people in the Holy Land itself, perhaps out of anger at the deception practiced upon him by Sunday school teachers in his youth. In Sunday school, he recalls, he had read about "All these kings," and imagined them "arrayed in royal robes ablaze with jewels," but on seeing them in their petty kingdoms, he finds only "ill-clad and ill-conditioned savages much like our Indians."²¹ When Twain's vendetta against James Fenimore Cooper for his idealizing the Indian is remembered, it is a wonder that Twain is no harder on Scripture and Sunday school teachers than he is in <u>Innocents Abroad</u>. Like the red man, Palestinians "were infested with vermin, and the dirt had caked on them till it amounted to bark."²² A daily scene, he declares,

> makes my flesh creep . . . a woman . . . with a child in her arms; honestly, I thought the child had goggles on as we approached . . . But when we drew near, we saw that the goggles were nothing but a camp-meeting of flies assembled around each of the child's eyes, and at the same time there was a detachment prospecting its nose. The flies were happy, the child was contented, and so the mother did not interfere.²³

Once more, Twain judges from the point of view of the civilized educated rationalist--there is no romanticism here, no Calvinism, no Christianity at all. From this enlightened stance Twain believes he discovers a source of Jesus's successful ministry in Palestine over eighteen centuries before. When a member of the American party, a physician named Dr. Birch, in an act of charity treats the fly-infested eyes of a child, the child's mother "started the whole nation" swarming around her and her baby: "the lame, the halt, the blind, the leprous, all the distempers . . . bred of indolence, dire, and iniquity-- . . . and still they came."²⁴ The way these creatures flocked about Dr. Birch suggested that they saw him as "gifted like a god," since each individual that got his portion of medicine grew radiant with joy and suffused this "thankless and impassive race [with] the unquestioning faith that nothing on earth could prevent the patient from getting well now." Twain speculates that much as these "sick people" flocked to our poor human doctor this morning . . . and worshipped him," their ancestors--"people precisely like them" . . . flocked in vast multitudes after Christ, and when they saw Him make the afflicted whole with a word . . . they worshipped Him."[25] This passage implies perhaps that Christ, in contrast to Dr. Birch, may not have been a "human doctor." But it is also possible to see the two healers as comparable: our human doctor was worshipped for his healing powers with medicine just as Christ was worshipped by these ignorant people of "unquestioning faith." It is inescapable that Twain's scepticism, his reasoning, and the evidence of his senses led him to a secular interpretation of the life of Jesus.

Such a view of Christ is encouraged by other events and views during the excursion. In Bethlehem, in the Church of the nativity, the party of eight pilgrims is shown the grotto below the manger where Christ was born. This is described by Twain as the "holiest ground on earth," yet he says "I touch, with a reverent finger, the actual spot where the infant Jesus lay, but I think nothing."[26] If, under these circumstances, Twain can "think" nothing and neglects to mention any feeling, which should precede thought, it is only fair to conclude that if only temporarily Sam Clemens does not accept the divinity of the place or the divinity of the story itself.

Among such disappointing phenomena Twain presents multiple views of the world, and his old device of dream and reality comes

53

into play. If he cannot believe in Christ's divinity by the light of day in Palestine's repulsive reality, he can dream of his acceptance of the Saviour by night:

> Night is the time to see Galilee . . . Gennesaret under these lustrous stars has nothing repulsive about it. Gennesaret with its glittering reflections of the constellations flicking its surfaces, almost makes me regret I ever saw the rude glare of day upon it . . . In the starlight, Galilee has no boundaries but the broad compass of the heavens, and is a theater meet for great events; meet for the birth of a religion able to save the world; and meet for the stately Figure appointed to stand upon its stage and proclaim its high decrees.[27]

Such a passage wishes to deny reality, the light of day, but of course cannot. It sees as a beautiful dream "a religion able to save the world." And here, it seems, is the point that Clemens came to and could not leave for the rest of his life. He could admire the message of the man who preached love and salvation for all and he could admire the power in the message, but he could not deny the reality of the light of day that rendered the message and the man who delivered it lost in an essentially secular world. In this respect, Clemens must be seen as denying the dream, denying the Romantic, though admitting its powerful appeal. Evidence of his suspension between two worlds comes from a notebook entry on the Holy Sepulcher written after the Palestine journey:

> Oh, for the ignorance & the confidingness of ignorance that could enable a man to kneel at the Sepulcher & look at the rift in the rock, & the socket of the cross & the tomb of Adam & feel & know & never question that they were genuine.[28]

As Ganzel has observed, Clemens felt keenly the loss of a "simple 'ignorant' faith."[29] To know, to feel, to never question--something he cannot do. When he finds himself "standing on the ground . . . once actually pressed by the feet of the Saviour" the "reality and a tangibility" of the scene are at odds with the . . . mystery and ghostliness that one naturally attaches to the character of a god. The mountains which that god looked upon, . . . surrounded by dusky men and women whose ancestors saw him, and even talked to him, face to face, . . . I cannot comprehend this."[30] Twain's failure to "comprehend" simply means that he cannot "know, feel, and never question." It is not God who has stood here but "a god." And these "dusky men and women" are ignorant descendants of ignorant ancestors. At this point Clemens would have to abandon the history he still carried with him of the man and his message. He would have to reassess it all to rediscover what was remarkable in both. Because what he saw was a barren, small part of the globe peopled by ignorant and ignoble people whose culture was to have given to the world a religion capable of saving that world. It was beyond belief to the rational, civilized, enlightened man. But it is important to see that Twain takes all of this very seriously and still longs for that "ignorant" faith. He is certainly not serious in his treatment of the unhistorical myths of Scripture. At the tomb of Adam he weeps to discover in this "land of strangers, far away from home . . . the grave of a blood relation."[31] He is utterly contemptuous of the bickering among the various priests who are required to approach the grave of the Saviour by different corridors "lest they quarrel and fight on the holiest ground on earth."[32] And he returns once more to his condemnation of organized Christianity, as he concludes his chapter on the Church of the Holy Sepulcher whose shrines "for fifteen hundred years . . . have been wet with the tears of pilgrims from the earth's remotest confines; for more than two hundred years, the most gallant knights that ever wielded sword wasted their lives" to "hold it sacred from infidel pollution." Recently a war costing "millions of treasure and rivers of blood, was fought between two rival nations claiming the sole right to put a new dome on it. History is full of this old Church . . . full of blood" shed out of the "respect and the veneration in which men held the last resting-place of the meek and lowly, the mild and gentle Prince of Peace!"[33] But this is an old point with Twain already--the inconsistency between the message and the practice of the Church. What is new is the shattered faith in an historical Jesus and an idealized Holy Land. The truthful reporter long suspected perhaps that he knew better than to believe the old Sunday school tracts, but in the absence of sensory evidence he had held those preconceptions to be true. And if the directors of the American Publishing Company in Hartford were hesitant to publish the book because of its "irreverent, even blasphemous . . . tone" and the very subtitle "The New Pilgrim's Progress" was a "sacrilege," yet Twain did not go so far in <u>Innocents Abroad</u> as to question outright the Bible's idea of God or the religious spirit. There is no evidence that these were dead for him at this time.

The next body of evidence in Clemens's spiritual development is the biographical material of his courtship of and marriage with Olivia Langdon after he came East in December 1866.

Van Wyck Brooks saw this marriage as the final misstep in Samuel Clemens's spiritual downfall; Olivia Langdon, he charged, was but a "passing reflection" of her acquisitive environment, and since Sam Clemens adored her as "little less than a saint," her gods became his gods.[34] In truth, the Langdons "moving in circles of small-town Protestant temperance," had "rather marked prejudices against alcohol and tobacco," were earnestly devoted to daily prayers and Bible-reading, and usually had a Congregational minister or two to Sunday dinner; yet in social sympathies the Langdons were liberal, having been active abolitionists before the Civil War as well as generous givers to the education of poor whites and blacks after the war.[35] Still, the Langdons were shocked at the idea of giving up their fragile, semi-invalid daughter to a brash Westerner who proposed to her the first time he visited their home and identified himself as a lost soul eager for her to Christianize. Clemens met the opposition to his courtship in correspondence to Livy and to others he believed capable of helping his cause. It is in this correspondence that he reveals his resistance to yet another attack on his heterodoxy.

In an early letter imploring Livy not to reject him out of hand, Clemens pleads to be corrected by Livy and Mrs. Fairbanks, a mutual acquaintance of his and the Langdons whom he had met aboard the Quaker City: "If you & Mother Fairbanks only scold me & upbraid now and then, I shall fight my way through the world, never fear." He promises to "try so hard to walk as you do, in the light and love of God," and ends one letter with, "Turn toward the Cross and be comforted--I turn with you."[36] Each week, as part of the spiritual instruction he is to receive at her hands, Clemens is to read the Bible, pray daily, and study the sermons of Henry Ward Beecher in the Plymouth Pulpit.[37]

It is possible, of course, to see Clemens as being entirely genuine in his expression of intent to try and "walk" in the light and love of God; it is, however, difficult to see him reading in good faith the sermons of Beecher or the Bible after his reaction to the Holy Land. The simple truth must be that Sam Clemens was in love and behaved no more rationally if somewhat more "honorably" than the Abelard he castigated for the seduction of Heloise. To his credit as an honest suitor, he confides to Livy in a letter written a month before their engagement February 4, 1869, some difficulty in his "self-regeneration." While admitting he is "dark" yet, he can see "the Saviour dimly at times."[38] A few weeks later he confesses:

> Oh it is slow and often discouraging . . . the emotion, the revealing religious emotions, Livy, will not come, it seems to me. I pray for it--it is all I can do. I do not know how to compel an emotion. And I pray every day that you may not be impatient or lose confidence in my final conversion. And I pray that my poisonous and besetting apathy may pass from me.[39]

It is possible that Clemens was trying here to return to a simple ignorant faith, but if he had earlier found no need for religion in "breadless times" it is also highly unlikely that he would have found a need for it in times when his heart was fully engaged by a woman he so obviously doted upon. Wecter believes that during these times Clemens came close to conversion " to please both Livy and Mrs. Fairbanks" but that the tone of his letters is that of a lover with "designs connubial" who shrewdly uses religious language calculated to advance his amorous cause.[40] If tone does not totally support Wecter's hypothesis, a letter written to his family in St. Louis the day after Clemens's engagement certainly does:

> She [Livy] said she never could or would love me--but she set herself the task of making a Christian out of me. I said she would succeed, but that in the meantime she would unwittingly dig a matrimonial pit & end by tumbling into it--& lo! the prophesy is fulfilled.[41]

It is obvious that the task Livy set herself is really one that Clemens urged upon her and that he deceived her further if he did indeed tell her she would succeed in making a Christian of him, for less than a month before their wedding he writes Livy that from reading he has found astronomy to be more "rational and believable than the Scriptures." The universe must be incalculably vaster and older, he believes, after he has compared astronomy's immensely enlarged cosmos with the Genesis account of creation. "In our pygmy little world!" we are but "an atom glinting with uncounted other myriads of other atom worlds in a broad shaft of light of God's countenance--and complacently prating of our speck as the Great World." He wonders whether Christ lived 33 years on each of the millions & millions of worlds that hold their majestic courses above our heads" and says he cannot "see how our astronomers can help feeling exquisitely insignificant, for the Book of the Heavens they open reveals that the world we are so proud of is to the universe of careening globes as is one mosquito to the winged & hoofed flocks & herds that darken the plains & the forests of all the earth. If you killed the mosquito would it be missed? Verily what is Man, that he should be considered of God?"[42] Once more, it is possible that Clemens is expressing an honest doubt introduced recently into his mind by a reading of astronomy, but there is no idea expressed here that he could not have picked up years before in his reading of Thomas Paine's <u>The Age of Reason</u>. His question of Christ living on each of millions of worlds is raised in "Captain Stormfield's Visit to Heaven," written almost two years before but constantly revised until it was published forty years later. Under any circumstances, Clemens does not finally deny the existence of God, rather he introduces Livy to what may very well be his concept of God at this time, a God of Paine, a god of reason, a god of Enlightenment.

Clemens probably fulfilled his reading assignments that Livy gave him and in rereading the Bible, as A. B. Paine observed, "from doctrinal point of view, as a guide to salvation," found "a large portion of it . . . absurd: a mass of fables, mere mythology."[43] At any rate, any change in religious belief or conduct that Clemens made in courting Livy lasted only a short time after they were married. He did not join the church as planned, or as he wrote his friend the Reverend Joe Twichell that he expected to do."[44] And sometime before the end of 1871, shortly after the marriage, the emphasis placed upon the daily Bible reading and prayers in the new household, according to Paine, brought forth Clemens's confessing to his wife:

> Livy, you may keep this [habit of daily Bible-reading] up if you want to, but I ask you to excuse me from it. It is making me a hypocrite. I don't believe in the Bible. It contradicts my reason. I can't sit here listening to it, letting you believe that I regard it, as you do, in the light of gospel, the word of God.[45]

And yet at this time Clemens was so in love with his wife that he could say, "I would deprive myself of sugar in my coffee if she wished it, or quit wearing socks if she thought them immoral."[46]

Thus in the final years of the 1860's, from his visit to the Holy Land, which tried whatever remained of his credibility in the historicity of Scriptures, through his courtship of Olivia Langdon, which challenged his apostasy from orthodoxy, Samuel Clemens was brought to the point where he confessed to his sister that he was at this time "an entire and absolute unbeliever."[47]

ENDNOTES TO CHAPTER III

1. Kenneth S. Lynn, <u>Mark Twain and Southwestern Humor</u> (Boston: Little, Brown, 1959), pp. 149-51.
2. <u>Innocents Abroad</u>, XI, 39.
3. <u>Innocents Abroad</u>, p. 40.
4. <u>Innocents Abroad</u>, p. 41.
5. <u>Innocents Abroad</u>, pp. 41-42.
6. <u>Innocents Abroad</u>, p. 209.
7. <u>Innocents Abroad</u>, p. 266.
8. <u>Innocents Abroad</u>, p. 266.
9. <u>Innocents Abroad</u>, p. 266.
10. <u>Innocents Abroad</u>, pp. 138, 139.
11. <u>Innocents Abroad</u>, p. 286.
12. <u>Innocents Abroad</u>, p. 286.
13. Allison Ensor, <u>Mark Twain and the Bible</u> (Lexington: University of Kentucky Press, 1969), p. 27.
14. <u>Innocents Abroad</u>, p. 237.
15. Cyril Clemens, <u>Wit and Wisdom</u> (New York: Frederick A. Stoakes Co., 1935), p. 15
16. <u>Innocents Abroad</u>, p. 232.
17. <u>Innocents Abroad</u>, p. 214.
18. <u>Innocents Abroad</u>, pp. 122, 123, 126.
19. <u>Innocents Abroad</u>, pp. 357, 358.
20. <u>Innocents Abroad</u>, p. 172.
21. <u>Innocents Abroad</u>, pp. 214-15.

22. *Innocents Abroad*, p. 199.
23. *Innocents Abroad*, pp. 199-200.
24. *Innocents Abroad*, p. 200.
25. *Innocents Abroad*, pp. 200-01.
26. *Innocents Abroad*, p. 351.
27. *Innocents Abroad*, pp. 244-45.
28. Dewey Ganzel, *Mark Twain Abroad; the Cruise of the Quaker City*, (Chicago: Univ. of Chicago Press, 1968), p. 250.
29. Ganzel, p. 250.
30. *Innocents Abroad*, p. 198.
31. *Innocents Abroad*, p. 307.
32. *Innocents Abroad*, p. 351.
33. *Innocents Abroad*, pp. 315-16.
34. Van Wyck Brooks, *The Ordeal of Mark Twain*, especially Chapter 5.
35. Wecter, *Love Letters*, pp. 62, 8.
36. Clara Clemens, *My Father, Mark Twain* (New York: Harper, 1931), pp. 20-21.
37. *Love Letters*, p. 9.
38. *Love Letter*, p. 45.
39. Caroline Thomas Harnsberger, *Mark Twain's Views on Religion* (Evanston, Ill.: Schori Press, 1961), p. 14.
40. Wecter, *Letters to Mrs. Fairbanks*, pp. xxviii, xxix.
41. *Love Letters*, p. 64.
42. *Love Letters*, pp. 133-34.
43. Paine, I, p. 411.

44. Frederick, <u>The Darkened Sky</u>, p. 141; <u>Letters to Mrs. Fairbanks</u>, p. 74.
45. Paine, I, p. 411.
46. <u>Paine</u>, I, p. 411.
47. Webster, <u>Mark Twain</u>: <u>Business Man</u>, p. 131. Webster assigns this letter to the early seventies.

CHAPTER IV: A LOOK BACK IN ANGER

By the 1870's Samuel Clemens has effectively resisted efforts to return him to the fold of orthodox Christianity even though he no doubt retained some prejudices from his Protestant childhood. But at the very time in his life when he recreates his lost Eden of Hannibal into the idyllic St. Petersburg of Tom Sawyer (1876), biographical and literary evidence reveals that his beliefs and attitudes are still changing. From his collaborative novel with Charles Dudley Warner The Gilded Age through the shorter satirical pieces The Curious Republic of Gondour and "Some Learned Fables for Good Old Boys and Girls" Twain reveals a beginning disillusionment with those Enlightenment beliefs that had easily sustained him while his old faith slipped from him, beliefs in the inherent decency and superiority of his nation and its institutions, political, economic, and ecclesiastical. He clearly discovers that the America he had used to show the corruption of the Old World in Innocents Abroad is itself quite corrupt.

Clemens's disillusionment with what he was to call the Gilded Age is first revealed in March, 1869 in a new Packard Monthly sermon-article entitled "Open Letter to Commodore Vanderbilt," New York City's current hero. Clemens responded to the unveiling of a statue of Vanderbilt and to the invocation given by the Right Reverend Bishop Janes who predicted that by amassing riches here below Vanderbilt had laid up "treasures in heaven." New York Mayor A. Oakley Hall exalted the honoree by comparing him to Franklin, Jackson, and Lincoln.[1] Such accolades were too much for Clemens. He wrote that Vanderbilt was "a rascal who had pillaged the nation and . . . been elevated to respectability," a man who had accumulated seventy million "greasy greenbacks." Yet to Clemens the real culprit was the acquisitive society which equated success with wealth to produce a cult that undermined the moral foundations of American democracy. Throughout his article, Twain addresses Vanderbilt as someone who needs to grasp the awful truth about himself, that countless anecdotes detail "your rise from penury to affluence, . . . praising you as if you were the last and noblest work of God, but unconsciously telling you how exquisitely mean a man has to be in order to achieve what you have achieved."[2]

Two and a half years later, September 27, 1871, Clemens contributes to the New York <u>Tribune</u> a second homiletic sketch in which again he indicts the very spirit of the Gilded Age by attacking the rascality of Boss William M. Tweed and his Tammany Ring as a reflection of the society they fleece out of millions. Calling his sketch the "First class in modern Moral Philosophy," Twain begins a dialogue:

>What is the chief end of men?
>
>A. To get rich.
>
>In what way?
>
>A. Dishonestly if we can; honestly if we must.
>
>Who is God, the one only and true?

> A. Money is God. Gold and greenbacks and stocks—father, son, and the ghost of the same—three persons in one: these are the true and only God, mighty and supreme; and William Tweed is his prophet.[3]

That Twain is not indicting something innate in man but a contemporary corruption is evident in the contrast he draws between the present and the past. Formerly, he says, the "works chiefly prized" were <u>Poor Richard's Almanac</u>, <u>The Pilgrim's Progress</u> and the <u>Declaration of Independence</u>. Now "the best prized Sunday-school books in this more enlightened age" are by the Ring members, including "St. Tweed's Handbook of Morals, and the Court-House edition of the Holy Crusade of the Forty Thieves."[4] It is worth noting that Twain sees collaboration between the institution of the Church in its Sunday school books and the corrupt city government.

Clemens's literary works of this period reveal the same sort of disillusionment with an economic system auspicious to "grab" mentality on both individual and national levels. Colonel Sellers says in <u>The Gilded Age</u>

> I go for putting the old flag on all the vacant lots. I said to the President, says I, 'Grant, why don't you take Santo Domingo, annex the whole thing, and settle the bill afterward?'[5]

And the Wall streeters behind Senator Dilworthy's shenanigans are typical of those preying upon the public trust through manipulation of their religious sympathies. When Harry Brierly goes to the Wall Street office of the president of the Columbus

River Slack Water Navigation Company to ask what happened to the money appropriated to dredge the Columbus River near Stone's Landing, the president tells him the first appropriation is already all gone: it was "a mere <u>initial</u> appropriation . . . never intended for anything but a mere nest egg for the future and <u>real</u> appropriations to cluster around." That "paltry" sum has been paid out in bribes to Congressmen, to lobbyists, and to popular religious journals for advertising. Dilworthy will get $10,000; a "high moral Congressman or Senator here and there--the high moral Congressman or Senator here and there--the high moral ones cost more, because they give tone to a measure." The president explains that he also appeals to the godly in his campaign for the <u>real</u> appropriation by planting favorable stories about the "improvement" in influential religious journals. As he proudly informs Brierly, "Perhaps the biggest thing we've done in the advertising line was to get an officer [who was highly placed in the U.S. government] to write up our little internal improvement for a religious paper of enormous circulation . . ." Then he comes to the point: the "religious paper" "is by far the best vehicle for a thing of this kind, because they'll 'lead' your article and put it right in the midst of the reading matter" with "a few Scripture quotations in it, and some temperance platitudes, and bit of gush here and there about Sunday-school . . . it works the nation like a charm" and no one realizes "that it is an advertisement." Others, "especially people who have got little financial schemes to make everybody rich," think the same way. "Of course, I mean your great big metropolitan religious papers that know how to serve God and make money at the same time . . ."[6]

Justin Kaplan called <u>The Gilded Age</u> "the most savage satire on democracy that American literature has to offer."[7] But such observations do not sound the depths of Clemen's revulsion, a revulsion fuelled by the betrayal of the principles taught him in Hannibal, principles of honor, decency, truth, and fair play. Clemens grew up in the New Eden of America, when the sense of Manifest Destiny was all around him, even in his own family, and when Hannibal leaned toward Know Nothingism. And if it is easy to see such thinking as chauvinistic and xenophobic in retrospect, Twain himself showed its positive side in writing of frontier villagers that though they were

> uncouth . . . they were honest and straightforward . . . Their patriotism was strong, their pride in the flag was of the old-fashioned pattern, their love of country amounted to idolatry. Whoever dragged the national honor in the dirt won their deathless hatred.[8]

This is an attitude apparent in Clemens himself in the writing he does from the Sandwich Islands and in <u>Innocents Abroad</u>. <u>The Gilded Age</u> is at least in part Clemens's recognition of the betrayal of those values of the "old-fashioned pattern" and imparts his disenchantment with his native land. And the arch betrayer is the congressman.

On March 10, 1873, in the New York <u>Tribune</u>, Twain writes, "To my mind Judas Iscariot was nothing but a low, mean, premature Congressman."[9] It is typical of his humor that Twain identifies the type by the name of Congressman and merely cites Iscariot as an example of the type. It is also evident that Twain is equating national issues in importance. Earlier in 1873 Twain wrote the <u>Tribune</u> on the annexation of the Hawaiian Islands: "We <u>must</u> annex these people," so that we can afflict them with our wise and beneficent government . . . introduce them to the novelty of thieves, . . . from street-car pick-pockets to municipal robbers and government defaulters." We must "show them how amusing it is to arrest them and then turn them loose--some for cause, and some for 'political influence.'" They can use "railway corporations who will buy their legislatures like old clothes, . . . We can furnish them some Jay Goulds who will do away with their old-time notion that stealing is not respectable."[10] His literary example of the arch betrayer is Senator Abner Dilworthy in <u>The Gilded Age</u> who corrupts government and betrays the people through total hypocrisy. In portraying this clever villain Twain is satirizing not just the nation's speculative frenzy, not just the governing body that can be bought and sold for hard cash, though both of these are obvious targets, rather he seeks to expose the trusted public official who uses the facade of religion as a weapon to put to sleep the faculties of a much-evangelized people by masquerading before them as a paragon of Christian virtue, while he slyly raids the national treasury with impunity.

On the Sunday before election day Dilworthy travels thirty miles in a rickety old stagecoach to the hamlet of Cattleville, to put his case before God and a Sunday-school gathering of farmers and their families assembled from miles around. His speech, Dilworthian to the core, reads like pure Americana. Using the third person, Dilworthy tells his rapt listeners of a Western lad born years ago, whose parents were so poor they "could not give him a costly education, but they were good and wise and sent him to Sunday-school." Later the good people of New Canaan made him governor--"all owing to the Sunday-school," as he says, and after that, they elected him a Representative to the Congress of the United States, where he grew famous. But in Congress he was tempted more than ever to go against his Sunday-school teaching--he naturally resisted all such temptations. Finally those same kind of people elevated him to "the towering, illustrious position . . . Senator of the United States!" Making use of two hoary rhetorical devices to end strong, Dilworthy withholds the name of the subject of his tale until the last and closes with a peroration of his theme. "That poor little boy that loved his Sunday-school became that man. <u>That man stands before you!</u> All that he is, he owes to the Sunday-school."[11]

This sermon conveys the Protestant ethic and patriotic formula for getting ahead in the Gilded Age: Don't drink, love-your-parents-and-country; be good to make good. But the speech is fraught with greater significance. Dilworthy is a full-blown portrait of the Sunday-school hero who winds up a rich and powerful guttersnipe in Congress by superficially conforming to the virtues espoused in Clemens's boyhood church literature.

Hollow to the core, Dilworthy's speech dupes the simple-minded religious fold who see in "a United States Senator a sort of god."[12]

Finally <u>The Gilded Age</u> seems to be illustrating the accuracy of the historian Charles Beard's description of the era, that it had the sort of government run "for the benefit of knaves at the expense of fools."[13] Yet Twain finds the church of his youth at least partially responsible for such knavery, in taking money for publishing immoral financial propaganda in its journals and in joining hands with evil by accepting words as deeds. Evil that once was destined for the eternal fires of hell now walks in the Sunday school mouthing religious platitudes; the forces of evil have appropriated the language of goodness as defined by small town American values. And Clemens becomes more outspoken in his attack on ministers of the church.

He was perturbed by the Reverend T. DeWitt Talmage, pastor of Brooklyn's Central Presbyterian Church who wanted to exclude common workingmen from his church because he said they smelled bad and would drive "the better class of worshippers away." Twain insisted upon reminding the Reverend precisely what Christianity was built upon. If Talmage's better class "had been chosen among the original Twelve Apostles he would not have associated with the rest," because of "the fishy smell of some of his comrades . . . from the Sea of Galilee. He would have resigned his commission" claiming "Master, if thou art going to kill the church thus with bad smells, I will have nothing to do with this work of evangelization."[14] And again in February, 1871 Twain attacked a New York Episcopalian rector named William T. Sabine for refusing to hold a burial service for an aged actor name George Holland because Holland's profession of playacting was immoral. Twain branded the refusal "a ludicrous satire upon Christian charity," and described the minister as a "giant of self-righteousness." He charged Sabine with violating "the letter of the Gospel" and the pulpit's mission of "disseminating the meat and marrow" of Christ's teachings from which, Twain observed, came "all that is great and good in our particular civilization." Unlike the stage, Twain noted, the pulpit "in its honest and well-meaning way . . . bores people with uninflammable truisms about doing good; bores them with correct compositions on charity' bores them, chloroforms, and stupefies them." "Ministers are not the only servants of God upon earth, nor His most efficient ones either . . ." and the "honorable George Holland" who "had for fifty years softened hard hearts, bred generosity in cold ones," had been "figuratively spit upon in his unoffending coffin by this crawling, slimy, sanctimonious, self-righteous reptile!" "The theatre teaches large audiences . . . 28 or 30 hours" a week "and the novelists and newspapers plead, and argue, and illustrate, stir, move, thrill, thunder, urge, persuade, supplicate, . . . millions and millions of people every single day." These media "till <u>nine-tenths</u> of the vineyard, and the pulpit tills the other tenth."[15] Obviously, Twain has not abandoned the Christian ethic in his attack upon churchmen;

rather he attacks churchmen for their abandoning the ethic they are committed to promulgate. Clemens sees clearly that the Church is but one of many institutions or forms by which the ethic can be disseminated and shows his impatience with its ineffectiveness in solving man's inhumanity to man, a problem he seems more and more concerned with in the 1870's.

In eight <u>Galaxy</u> articles on Chinese persecution as he recalled witnessing it, Twain shows evidence of emerging from the racial and religious bigotry that had earlier comprised his Americanism. His first contribution on the subject, "Disgraceful Persecution of a Boy," evokes the bitter recollection when as a reporter in San Francisco he saw Irish "hoodlums" stone a Chinese laundryman just for kicks, only to have <u>Call</u> editor, George E. Barnes, kill his account of the incident. Of this incident, Clemens said,

> By my Presbyterian training I knew that the <u>Morning Call</u> had brought disaster upon itself. I knew the ways of Providence and I knew that this offense would have to be answered for.[16]

Such a reflection on Clemens's part suggests that though he had given up belief in religion, he retained the notion of divine retribution while he was still in California--something nowhere evident in the Masonic or Deistic beliefs he was then supposedly holding but a holdover from his more primitive Calvinistic beliefs that subsequent events would not substantiate. At any rate, the persecuting "boy" who participated in the stoning was, according to Twain, presumably an Irish lad and thus trained to mistreat the Chinese; he was simply following community mores when he threw stones at them, for the boy knew full well that a Chinese "has no rights that any man was bound to respect; no sorrows that any man was bound to pity;" his life and his liberty were worthless "when a white man needed a scapegoat; . . . individuals, communities, the majesty of the State itself, joined in hating, abusing, and persecuting these humble strangers. And therefore," it was but natural "for this sunny-hearted boy, tripping along to Sunday school with his mind teeming with freshly-learned incentives to high and virtuous action, to say to himself: 'Ah, there goes a Chinaman! God will not love me if I do not stone him.'" Yet, as Twain concludes, the "poor chap" was cruelly arrested and jailed for this, even though "Everything conspired to teach him that it was a high and holy thing to stone a Chinaman."[17] Twain tries to evoke shame in those participating in the oppression or degradation of the New York City Chinese who are treated but little better than the San Francisco laundryman, and his examples are often so extreme that they become melodramatic. But by describing such atrocities, real or imagined, Clemens shows a growing skepticism about the possibilities of his own society being "reasoned." He is clearly seeing that the degradation is not limited to the Old World, is not restricted to the ignorant and the poor of the Holy Land, but is a part of the American way of life supported by church and government. He is, in fact, moving closer toward nineteenth century science's conception of man in an alien universe that will take shape in the first formulation of his vaunted bitter philosophy of the 1800's.

In the 1870's Clemens recorded what he liked as a reader: "I like history, biography, travels, curious facts and strange happenings, and science," and as Waggoner pointed out, Clemens was acquainted with the theory of organic evolution even before he read Darwin and understood enough about the astronomical geological speculations to grasp the New Science's "time-scale that dwarfs all human history and makes individual human life so insignificant as to be invisible to the observer accustomed to the majestic pulses of geologic time."[18] Clemens easily turned such speculation into a cause-effect chain. "The first act of that first atom" floating on the Laurentian sea "led to the second act of the first atom, and so on down through the succeeding ages of all life." If the process "could be traced," we would see "that the first act of that first act has led inevitably to the act of my standing here in my dressing gown at this instant talking to you."[19] Such ideas from his reading now doubtless strengthened the rational side of this nature that Clemens had cultivated since the 1850's when he read The Age of Reason, just as later readings in Darwin, Huxley, and Haeckel would move him toward his so-called air-tight determinism.[20] He used ideas from Darwin and his interpreters to reinforce his dismal conclusion that "the universe and man are of one piece, and both are mechanisms; man is a pitiable creature, nothing but an aggregate of mechanisms, nothing but an animal; a single human being, all of human history even, is infinitely unimportant in the vastness of an impersonal universe."[21] And some of Twain's work from the 1870's suggests such a view of life at this time.

As religious satire, Twain's minor sketch titled "Some Learned Fables for Good Old Boys and Girls" (1874) deserves a closer look than critics have given it. In this obviously futuristic piece, insects who now dominate the earth are on a scientific excursion led by the Duke of Longlegs to venture beyond the forest and "out into the unknown and unexplored world" believed by some of their researchers to have once been occupied by Mankind. Enroute they engage in reflections upon God and religion. Most evident in the sketch is the outright ridicule that Twain aims at missionaries. For example, after finding a foreign country of a dark-skinned, timid, gentle race of spiders who are "ignorant and heathenish worshippers of unknown Gods," the expedition acts in the approved nineteenth-century Protestant crusader's style and sends out "a great detachment of missionaries to teach them the true religion."

> . . . in a week's time a precious work had been wrought among those darkened creatures, not three families being by that time at peace with each other or having a settled belief in any system of religion whatever.[22]

The dedicated insect missionaries like the Protestant missionaries Clemens had seen in Hawaii, had undermined their "heathen" insects' faith, but without supplanting it with their own. Yet they were not discouraged by failure, for ironically "This . . . encouraged the expedition to establish a colony of missionaries there permanently that the work of grace might go on."[23] Their evangelism does not have to make sense for the zealots to continue it.

Frederick believes that Twain's chief target in "Fables" relates directly to Twain's Calvinist origins and a belief in "debased" human nature. The wood creatures are stupid and perhaps depraved, certainly they are arrogant, but the "ignorant and heathenish" spiders are timid, gentle, and definitely not depraved and clearly do not represent a separate species. The wood creatures themselves are "long-legs" (spiders), "snail" (crustacean), etc. Thus the satire cannot hold all mankind depraved, as Frederick implies, but only "civilized" mankind, a view that is not Calvinistic but Romantic.

The satirical allegory is made more difficult by the implied search to determine, once the remains of Man show him to be not mythical, what is man?, perhaps Twain's earliest attempt to answer this question in a piece of published writing. Professor Woodlouse writes of the evidence of man's killer-instinct and bizarre religious customs showing the primitive creature to have been "a companion of the other low orders of life that belonged to that forgotten time . . . the mastodon, the ichthyosaurus." On man's religion specifically, he concludes that this human ancestor apparently believed in God and the soul. . . . [at least] he imagined he had a soul, and pleased himself with the fancy that it was immortal."[25] Such a view of man is indeed Calvinistic, but Woodlouse is inaccurate in dating man as belonging to only a prehistoric time, unless the wood creatures mean by prehistoric a time preceding their own histories. Can he therefore be believed?

Longlegs concludes--upon mistaken evidence--that "instead of being the ignorant savage reptile we have been taught to consider him, [man] was creature of cultivation and high intelligence."[26] This view is non-Romantic, non-Calvinistic and very much an Enlightenment view applauding civilization. Thus Frederick could only arrive at his conclusion that the satire is Calvinistic by taking Woodlouse's view of man and by rejecting the benevolent spiders as of the same "species" with the other wood creatures. What is most clear is that Twain satirizes in detail the institutions of civilization and the arrogance of that civilization. He is warming in this for the work to be done in Tom Sawyer. It is not clear that Twain sides finally with the Calvinists or with the scientific determinists who see man as a depraved victim of forces over which he has no control. Twain often suggests such ideas, but he never believes for long that mankind is past redemption or that mankind is not eligible for redemption. Thus despite the worst he could say against a theology he had outgrown, he set out in his satire to ridicule mankind into living up to an honor and a dignity in keeping with non-Calvinistic conceptions of mankind, for it must be seen that Clemens's deterministic conception is no more than science's fitting itself to a Calvinistic concept of depravity. Though Clemens found science documenting concepts he claims to have set aside, their appeal is evident. Still, it must not be supposed that he rested content in them, for there was by now working within him the notion of man's higher possibilities, an innate divinity almost, there to redeem him, a romantic view of man and the universe coexisting with the Calvinistic scientific construct. The deterministic view of man is every bit as much dream as it is reality. Clemens's quarrel at this point is with a church that is dry and lifeless in its rituals, a church that ignores evil in the world, a church that through its literature oversimplifies the complexities of existence, and promotes a distorted view of the world in its congregation--accepting the Dilworthies as virtuous because they give lip service to the church and continue to wreak havoc among mankind. He is angry at a government that is impervious to right and wrong and a constituency that is ignorant and unreasoning in allowing its government and its churches to rob it of dignity and value.

At this point Clemens's position seems decidedly more Enlightenment than it does either Romantic or Calvinistic. The wood creatures of the "Fables" and the dupes of <u>The Gilded Age</u> are absurd not because they were born innately depraved or have been victimized by the corrupt institutions of civilization, but because they have departed from "right reason." Clemens seems to have moved from Calvinism fully into the intellectual stance of Thomas Paine in <u>The Age of Reason</u> but not yet far enough to be a full fledged scientific determinist. Yet it is a stance he cannot wholly abandon even as he moves toward romanticism in <u>Tom Sawyer</u>.

For someone who has seen no need for religion and someone

who cannot accept the Bible, who has become the secular man, Clemens has found no faith in government at any level and nothing in the Church as a social institution. In truth the only secular faith left to him would have been the family and some notion of the perfectibility of man, if he still held to some of his deistic beliefs. Nothing, however, indicates that Clemens is at odds with the universe nor with the will that moves it. In fact, his condemnation only makes sense when predicated on the idea of human capacity for change.

ENDNOTES TO CHAPTER IV

1. Foner, pp. 156, 157.
2. Foner, p. 157; see also *Mark Twain: Life As I find It*, edited by Charles Neider (Garden City, New York: Hanover House, 1961), pp. 38-42 (p. 38).
3. The references to "A Revised Catechism" are to a reprint in Arthur L. Vogelback's "Mark Twain and the Tammany Ring," *PMLA*, Vol LXX (March 1955), 69-77. See pages 72-76 for the reprinted sketch.
4. "A Revised Catechism," p. 76.
5. *The Gilded Age*, Vol. II, pp. 79-80.
6. *The Gilded Age*, Ch. 28, Vol. I, pp 276-279.
7. Introduction to *The Gilded Age* (New York: Trident Press, 1964), p. vii.
8. *The Gilded Age*, Vol. II, p. 49.
9. Arthur L. Vogelback, "Mark Twain: Newspaper Contributor," *American Literature*, Vol. 20 (May 1948), 111-28 (p. 113).
10. *Vogelback*, p. 123.
11. *The Gilded Age*, Vol. II, p. 220.
12. *The Gilded Age*, Ch. 22, Vol. II, p. 215.
13. Gladys Bellamy, *Mark Twain Literary Artist*, p. 293.
14. *Contributions to the Galaxy*, 1870-1871, by Mark Twain, ed. Bruce R. McElderry (Gainesville, Florida: Scholars' Facsimiles and Reprints, 1961), p. 42.
15. *Contributions to the Galaxy*, pp. 128-29.

16. Neider, <u>Autobiography</u>, p. 122.

17. <u>Contributions to the Galaxy</u>, p. 43.

18. Hyatt Howe Waggoner, "Science in the Thought of Mark Twain," <u>American Literature</u>, Vol. 8 (Jan. 1937), 357-70 (pp. 362, 359).

19. Paine, I, 397.

20. Waggoner, pp. 364-67; S. Leacock, <u>Mark Twain</u> (New York: D. Appleton and Co., 1933), pp. 18, 19, 147-49.

21. <u>Waggoner</u>, p. 36.

22. Twain, <u>Sketches, New and Old</u>, p. 153.

23. <u>Sketches, New and Old</u>, p. 153.

24. Frederick, p. 149.

25. <u>Sketches, New and Old</u>, p. 161.

26. <u>Sketches, New and Old</u>, pp. 164-65.

CHAPTER V: ROMANCE AND DETERMINISM

Between <u>Tom Sawyer</u> (1876) and his masterpiece, <u>Huckleberry Finn</u> (1884), Samuel Clemens became a harassed husband enmeshed in the varied activities of author, publisher, and speculator that he pursued to support an expensive household in early suburbia. During these eight years he turned out almost a book a year, a good deal of journalistic hackwork and several sketches, all of which provide evidence of a thoroughly inconsistent view of the universe ranging from Romantic optimism to naturalistic despair.

To DeVoto, <u>Tom Sawyer</u> is "the supreme American idyll,"[1] and to Maxwell Geismar an "edenic vision" when "village society . . . has not yet been converted to the rationale of work, social respectability, and material success." Geismar points out that "in this boyhood idyll of freedom from civilization . . . we come finally to the symbol of absolute-freedom"--Huck Finn.[2] Henry Nash Smith observes that for a century, thousands of readers have found in the novel a picture of "Natural man beleaguered by society, but able to gain happiness by escaping to the forest and the river." In such a conflict, Smith reasons, nineteenth-century writers echo the tradition of the Romantics and identify themselves with the virtuous hero and "ascribe evil exclusively to society." Smith argues against such a romantic interpretation by showing that Twain appears throughout on the side of his protagonist but that he still does not paint the institutions of school and church as "truly evil"--they are simply boring. Tom never intends "running away for good" from the fetters of civilization, but childishly indulges in self-pity, just as in playing pirate he was acting out a "child's fantasy."[3]

So Smith infers that Tom achieves the best of both worlds. He defies society and yet retains not only its acceptance but its adulation. Smith's view seems a fairly accurate one. In keeping Tom as his hero rather than Huck, who clearly represents total freedom, Twain is not working from a totally romantic stance. Indeed Blair sees the development of the novel as moving Tom from an irresponsible mischief-maker toward a more mature and responsible adult. It is true that in the last chapters Twain does not employ so "simple and melodramatic a device as a complete reformation," yet he does show that Tom not only acts grownup but accepts "the adult code of the particularly godly fold of idyllic St. Petersburg."[4] Indeed at the end, the anti-Sunday school hero demonstrates pretty conclusively that he has come to terms with Main Street-St. Petersburg, for the last time we see him in action, he is using his wiles to convert Huck back to the respectability of the Widow Douglas's household.

Certainly in the presentation of his characters in Tom Sawyer, Twain often suggests a romantic stance as he does in portraying the dull ritual and restraints of the church. In fact, the novel almost implies that "good" is unnatural, is the result of restraint and constraint. Thus Tom is wicked in that he cannot easily or superficially accept the constraints. So Tom hates Willie Mufferson because ". . . he is so good." But Twain is careful that we know Willie takes "as good care of his mother as if she were cut glass."[5] The point is that Willie's mother does not need caring for, that Willie's attentions are thus unnatural. Willie does what the civilized Sunday school adult world demands.

Tom's foster-mother Aunt Polly is faced with the same division between the "good" and the natural as she reveals in thinking aloud about her foster child. In "sparing the rod and spoiling the child," she knows she's "laying up sin and suffering" for both of them. "He's full of the Old Scratch, but laws-a-me! he's my own dead sister's boy, poor thing, and I ain't got the heart to lash him, somehow." When she lets him off, "my conscience does hurt me so, and everytime I hit him my old heart most breaks. Well-a-well," she concludes, "man that is born of woman is of few days and full of trouble as the Scripture says . . ."[6] Four of Aunt Polly's five sentences refer directly to Scripture or to "sin." Clearly hers has been a Calvinistic indoctrination. The notion of innate depravity is implicit in the idea that children who are not beaten are "spiled," thus they are born inclined toward evil. That the boy is innately depraved is suggested by his being "full of the Old Scratch," something he could not at his early age be expected to have absorbed from a Christian environment, home, community. The bleakness of a Calvinistic view is evident in the lines from Ecclesiastes--life is short and "full of trouble." All of this Aunt Polly has been taught; it is what her "conscience" tells her, the conscience that "hurts" when she "lets him off." Her heart, on the other hand, that natural, innate entity so at odds with conscience, asks her not to "lash" the boy, and almost breaks when she does. So Aunt Polly is torn by what society-conscience demands and what nature-heart demands. And clearly Twain would have us condemn the demands of society-conscience here. Thus, there is at least in this passage, a preference for the romantic's view of the superiority of heart or feelings determining human actions over the Calvinist's notions of innate depravity.

In other ways, Twain encourages a Romantic interpretation of <u>Tom Sawyer</u>. The reference to the German boy who had "once recited three thousand verses without stopping; but the strain upon his mental faculties was too great, and he was little better than an idiot from that day forth . . ."[7] suggests that memorizing verses or any other sort of severe mental effort is unnatural. The dryness and sterility of school and Sunday school suggest that vitality lies outside the confines of both institutions. Neither is evil in itself, but neither has positive value.

If the novel is treated as an idyll, and this is a sound way of looking at it, a story of a life that is no more, a life that has passed, there is nothing that says the past celebrated is the first half of the nineteenth century. In the total freedom of Huck Finn is seen a prelapsarian condition no longer possible. The mothers of the town hate and dread Huckleberry Finn, "because he was idle and lawless and bad--and because all their children admired him . . . delighted in his forbidden society, and wished they dared to be like him." Huck comes and goes of "his own free will." "He didn't have to go to school or church, or call any being master or obey anybody;" he fished "when and where he chose, . . . as long as it suited him; nobody forbade him to fight; he could sit up as late as he pleased; he was always the first" to go "barefoot in the spring and the last to resume leather in the fall; he never had to wash, nor put on clean clothes; he could swear wonderfully. In a word, everything that goes to make life precious, that boy had. So thought every harassed, hampered respectable boy in St. Petersburg."[8] Huck is "free"; his will is free; he is free from work ("idle")--which society has forbidden in the so-called work ethic. He is free from law ("lawless")--which society has imposed to limit that freedom. He is free from conscience ("bad")--thus he is "hated and dreaded by all the mothers of the town." "Everything that goes to make life precious, that boy had. So thought every harassed, hampered respectable boy in St. Petersburg." Tom Sawyer is a harassed, hampered respectable boy. But Huck himself is in some ways as Melville says of Billy Budd, "a sort of upright barbarian, such as Adam was before the fall." Twain would seem to be saying this was what it was like, this is what man was, but there has been the fall and this can be no more. In other words, at one time, nature sufficed, man was born basically good, but man became a "social animal"--he fell from Eden into society, into self-consciousness.

Enter Tom Sawyer. It is noteworthy that when Tom hears anything in the sermon at the church he attends, it is the minister's stirring picture of Doomsday: ". . . the assembling together of the world's host at the millennium when the lion and the lamb should lie down together and a little child should lead them."[9] It is significant that the Calvinistic doom passes Tom completely by. Instead he picks up on the only egocentric thing he can make of the message and "wished that he could be that child, if it was a tame lion."[10] The idea of an innate depravity of man is seemingly irrelevant to the boy. Twain seems to be pointing out that not only are church and school dull, they do not do their work, they do not make a lasting impression. There are, of course, the "good" boys, but that goodness is superficial, not genuine, and in their heart of hearts these respectable boys admire Huckleberry Finn. Girls, of course, are born civilized.

One further passage, an exchange between Tom and Huck, raises an interesting point. Geismar claims that through Huck "we get the sense of that darker stream of Negro superstitiousness, of African witchcraft, of voodoo charms and cures which runs, like a submerged Mississippi current, through the pages of *Tom Sawyer*."[11] But it is Tom who argues that the howling of a stray dog at night over the sleeping Muff Potter after the murder of Dr. Robinson, portends Potter's certain death, and Huck who points out that

> . . . they say a stray dog come howling around Johnny Miller's house 'bout midnight, as much as two weeks ago; . . . and there ain't anybody dead there yet."
> "Well, I know that. And suppose there ain't. Didn't Gracie Miller fall in the kitchen fire and burn herself the very next Saturday?"
> "Yes, but she ain't <u>dead</u>. And what's more, she's getting better, too."
> "All right, you wait and see. She's a goner, just as sure as Muff Potter's a goner. That's what the niggers say, and they know all about these kind of things, Huck."[12]

In some ways Huck's refusing superstition when it conflicts with his experience is characteristic of his practical perception of reality, and Tom's insistence upon superstition and his bending evidence to reinforce it is characteristic of an adult. Thus the natural man, if this is what Huck represents, rejects anything contrary to experience, and Tom, the "good hearted but still civilized" boy will reject experience in the light of authority. Tom relies very heavily upon the authority of "books" in developing the rules for pirate gangs.

But Twain is not this consistent in working out what the boys stand for, or rather he is more realistic than allegorical in showing inconsistencies within his characters, as the midnight discussion between Tom and Huck near the grave of Hoss Williams reveals:

> "Say, Hucky--do you reckon Hoss Williams hears us talking?"
> "O'course he does. Least his spirit does."
> Tom, after a pause:
> "I wish I'd said Mister Williams. But I never meant any harm. Everybody calls him Hoss."
> "A body can't be too partic'lar how they talk about these yer dead people, Tom."[13]

It can be argued, of course, that Huck has no experience with which to refute such superstition, but here he seems to know and

Tom seems to not know. It is characteristic of Tom that he wishes he had used "Mister," as though the niceties of society are the crucial thing.

So in <u>Tom Sawyer</u>, there is a clearly implied rejection of the Calvinistic doctrine of innate depravity of all mankind--it may apply to Injun Joe, but it is definitely not applied to the "damned human race." There is a clearly implied rejection of "civilizing" or Enlightenment positive forces--church and school, not to condemn them as evil, but simply showing them as unimportant. And there is much to encourage a romantic view in the novel. But the fact remains that Tom, not Huck, is the hero of the novel, and Tom, though he has been bored by both church and Sunday school and has chafed under the civilizing restraints of Aunt Polly and his cousin Mary, is still partially civilized, certainly more civilized than Huck. Tom is accepted and finally respected by the civilized society that Huck as natural man is indifferent to, at least in <u>Tom Sawyer</u>.

Where this leads in exploring Clemens's religious stance at this time is fairly clear. Orthodoxy is boring. The mechanistic laws of nature created by a god of reason seem inapplicable. Man is born predominantly good through the offices of a beneficent deity. If it is argued that <u>Tom Sawyer</u> is finally no more than idyll, Twain's fantasy, "The Facts Concerning the Recent Carnival of Crime in Connecticut," published in the same year as <u>Tom Sawyer</u>, reinforces some of the same ideas found in the novel.

Twain's "Carnival" fantasy takes as its subject the warfare

between the sketch's narrator and his self-styled "trained Presbyterian conscience," which in the fable torments him so relentlessly that he is driven to murder it. One morning when the narrator sits in his study anticipating a visit from his Aunt Mary, he is so elated at the prospect that he says to himself, "If my most pitiless enemy could appear before me at this moment, I would freely admit any wrong I had done him." At that very moment, the narrator's Conscience enters the door and proceeds with "exquisite cruelty" to torture him. "Every sentence was an accusation, and every accusation a truth [that] burned like vitriol."[14] With mounting exasperation, he asks, "Is there any way of satisfying that malignant invention which is called a conscience?" The answer he receives is an emphatic no: "I don't care," he is told, "what act you may turn your hand to, I can straightway whisper a word in your ear and make you think you have committed a dreadful meanness. It is my business--and my joy--to make you repent everything you do." The desperate narrator agrees with this inner monster wholeheartedly: "Don't worry, you haven't missed a trick. . . . I never did a thing in my life, virtuous or otherwise, that I didn't repent of in twenty-four hours."[15] Finally he murders his conscience and exclaims wildly that he is at last a free man, "a man WITHOUT A CONSCIENCE!"[16] He proceeds to celebrate his freedom by indulging in an orgy of crime with what he calls "unalloyed bliss."

In modern terminology, as Lynn observes, Clemens meant by conscience "something vaguely like what we would call the superego." Lynn proceeds to quote Clemens's own statement from an unpublished notebook: "Conscience is . . . moral, not physical. . . . It is merely a thing: the creature of training; it is whatever one's mother and Bible and comrades and system of government and habitat and heredities have made it. . . . Inborn nature is Character by itself in the brutes--the tiger, the dove, the fox, etc. Inborn nature and the modifying Conscience, working together make Character in man."[17] For this definition to make sense, Twain must mean by "heredities" not genetically transmitted qualities but qualities inherent in given environment, as distinct from "inborn nature," that which is innate. If this sketch is allegorical, by extending the allegory it is possible to see that when conscience in "killed," the remaining "inborn nature" that remains goes on a crime spree. Thus "inborn nature" would be Calvinistically depraved. But it is not clear that this was Clemens's intent.

Geismar's interpretation of this "savage fantasy" leans toward Otto Rank's "depth psychology." The fable, Geismar declares, reveals in its author "a soul both pagan and civilized," and the one did not replace the other but fused with it to create Clemens's "central artistic vision"; thus it is a fable of "the hero's liberation from the repressive burden of civilizational discontents. . . . his determination to be himself at all cost"--just as every artist yearns to be.[18] Geismar would thus see the allegory as completed when the conscience is killed; the artist must free himself of the useless conventions of society to find his natural self. And the "Fable" supports such a view. After committing moral mayhem, the narrator says, "I settled all my old outstanding scores, and began the world anew."[19] To create the world anew, to return to Adam before the fall, but his is done only after "settling all my old outstanding scores," which could only be done after conscience has been destroyed.

Clearly for Clemens conscience is more than anything else the source of guilt--not simply that which tells him a particular act is wrong or that another act is right and good. For Clemens, Conscience here seems the equivalent of guilt--that which Jonathan Edwards considered "natural to man," but which Clemens saw as a consequence of training. It is important that Tom Sawyer has small attacks of it, but almost only when he feels he has hurt those close to him. He is impervious to the conscience taught in church or school. Certainly if guilt--the necessary consequence of innate depravity (man born evil and incapable on his own of any good since good can come only through God acting upon man and God acts only upon the elected few)--is the equivalent of Conscience, the "Fable" must be read as a rejection of Calvinism. But Geismar in calling the piece a "savage fantasy" may be completely accurate. Clemens may have felt, and often indicated he did feel, that conscience was inimical to happiness, and he may have wanted to destroy it, but it is not so easily done. "Fable" is a fantasy, not an autobiography. Clemens has not laid the ghost of conscience, nor has he secured the headstone on guilt's grave.

A notebook entry from 1895 sheds a good deal of light on Clemens's conception of conscience:

> . . . in a crucial moral emergency a sound heart is a safer guide than an ill-trained conscience. I sh'd support this doctrine with a chapter of a book of mine where a sound heart and a deformed conscience come into collision and conscience suffers defeat. Two persons figure in this chapter: Jim, a middle-aged slave, and Huck Finn, a boy of 14.[20]

By refusing to use "heart" without the qualifier "sound," Clemens leaves open the possibility of an "unsound" or "depraved" heart, and since consciences can be either "ill-trained" or otherwise, we can infer that some conscience can be "well-trained"; thus conscience is not an evil in itself; hearts are not the result of training and may possibly be innately unsound or depraved. Such a passage seems to leave all the doors open to a view of man that is neither totally romantic, Calvinistic, nor Enlightenment. Any romantic would admit without question that the "heart" is a safer guide than "conscience" as Clemens construed the latter word. Any good practicing mind in the Enlightenment would have argued that a well-trained conscience--again as Clemens understood the word--is a safe guide in a moral emergency. A good Calvinist would have known that there is no such thing as a "sound" heart without the sanctifying grace of God. But Clemens's qualifiers keep him from clearly inhabiting any single camp.

The second of the three sketchers, "Some Rambling Notes," may be no more than a classification of religious "types," but it does reveal some of Clemens's religious preoccupations at this time. The first type is the hypocritical, greedy, sanctimonious, materialist found in Twain's earlier indictment of the gilded age, but the second type provides evidence of Clemens's continuing fascination with the idea of predestination. The "Reverend" narrator in the yarn relates an incident of a shipwrecked group of people who drift on a raft for eight days in the cold mid-Atlantic, without provisions or adequate clothing finally seeing their last chance, a ship, "gliding relentlessly from them." Though they have lost their voices, each one then "knelt at the base of the oar that was waving the signal-coat aloft. . . . The sea was tossing; the sun rested, a red, rayless disk on the sea-line in the west. . . . the ship's sails lay wrinkled and flapping against her masts--she was going about" and they are saved. The Reverend builds up his tale into a sermon as he proclaims the Presbyterian gospel that all this has been predestined:

> There was one little moment of time in which that raft could be visible from that ship, and only one. If that one little fleeting moment had passed unfruitful, those men's doom was sealed. As close as that does God shave events foreordained from the beginning of the world.[21]

In this portrait there is no religious cant or hypocrisy, no use of empty scriptural phrases to justify immoral greed. Instead there is an attempt to see the use which one man puts religion to--explaining fate. That Clemens himself never completely escaped a mechanistic conception of the universe perhaps lends a dignity to this portrait.

A third and final yarn from "Some Rambling Notes" is related about the late Captain "Hurricane" Jones of the Pacific Ocean, "a rather severe satire on modern scientific religionists." Sincerely pious, the Captain prides himself on being a Biblical scholar and believes everything in the Bible, although he "applied natural laws to the interpretation of its miracles." The Captain explains the miracle of Elijah (whom the Captain mistakenly calls Isaac) and the prophets of Baal. At a time in Israel, the Captain says, when the heathen prophets "took all the trade" and the "Christian's" stock had sunk pretty low, Isaac challenges the prophets to "pray down fire on an alter." The prophets take up the challenge and pray "till they were all tuckered out, and they owned up and quit." In his turn, Isaac asks some friends to pour water on the altar and then prays an endless Presbyterian prayer "about the heathen in distant lands, and about the sister churches, and about the state and the country at large . . ." Finally, "when nobody was watching" Isaac puts a lighted match to the liquid, and "pff! up the whole thing blazes like a house afire!" What the spectators did not know, explains the Captain, was that the water poured on the altar of Isaac's friends was "Petroleum, sir PETROLEUM!" So, the Captain concludes, "There ain't a thing in the Bible but what is true; all you want to do is to go prayerfully to work and cipher out how 'twas done."[22]

The Captain, working from the assumption of the truth of Scripture, must contend with apparent contradictions. He resolves them by interpreting the Scripture in the light of the known present--something that will later remove him from the "literal" school of fundamentalism. That Twain notes the Captain "swears" but is deeply pious is an interesting inversion of the earlier types, the hypocrites who appropriate the words of piety but are essentially obscene or profane in spirit. And that the Captain is "a rather severe satire on modern scientific religionists" suggests that in this gallery of religious types there is nothing to which Clemens can claim to be his own. He is the observer, detached, amused, scornful, sympathetic, but quite clearly uncommitted.

A third piece from this period, the short story "The Great Revolution in Pitcairn" (1878), develops Clemens's growing concern with the lethal combination of piety and ignorance worked in The Gilded Age. The revolutionists, descendants of the Bounty crew, have been led into throwing off "the galling English yoke," even though they swear it has never galled them before, by Butterworth Stavely, an American who had come to the island only four months before and found the islanders' sole occupations to be farming and fishing, "their sole recreation, religious services." Stavely is crowned Emperor Butterworth I and begins "imperial reforms." He creates a nobility, a standing army and navy and gives Biblical names to his appointees--the Grand Duke of Galilee, Minister of War; the Duke of Bethany, Post-master-general; the Viscount of Canaan, etc. But friction begins when Stavely levies intolerable taxes "to support the army, the navy, and the rest of the imperial establishment." Finally, in church on Sunday morning, with the army at his back, he commands "the ministry of the treasury to take up collection" and the revolution breaks out, restores the former regime, and condemns Stavely "to perpetual banishment from church services, or to perpetual labor as galley slave in the whale-boat--whichever [he] might prefer."[23]

Budd sees this piece as political satire reflecting Twain's "first predictions that the New World was drifting toward chaos."[24] Blair judges the tale's pessimism to be more inclusive: "Twain . . . meant this little tale to be a history of civilization in miniature." That is, Stavely as civilization's instigator comes to an island like "the tranquil Hannibal" of young Clemens, remote from a troubled world and "plays on secret desires . . . uses arguments calculated to sway dull-minded people," and since human beings like Stavely with mean motives and those like the stupid islanders form the great majority, Stavely achieves his unholy ends--"anything but an admirable spectacle" of mankind.[25]

Certainly, Twain shows the jeopardy the islanders put themselves in by being ignorant and blindly pious--taking the religious word for the moral deed, but it is in no way clear that the final message of the tale is pessimistic. After all, the islanders do reject Stavely and restore their civilization. The piece is neither totally pessimistic nor Calvinistic. Rather it seems to show that governments and churches are poor expedients of and for both the unenlightened and the opportunistic. It is not indeed "an admirable spectacle," it is most unromantic, but it is most un-Calvinistic as well; neither does it verify the stance of the man of the Age of Reason.

That Clemens no longer seems to accept the principles of the Enlightenment, of Deism, is an extremely important point here because almost everything he said at about this time points to such a view of the world--a God of Reason creating through immutable laws of Reason and Nature a world governed by those laws in men born neither innately good nor evil but with the capacity for reason to live in accordance with those laws. Writing on the human idea of God, old and new, he could say:

> The difference in importance, between the God of the Bible and the God of the present day, cannot be described. . . . one cannot put the modern heavens on a map, nor the modern God; but the Bible God and the Bible heavens can be set down on a slate, . . .
> The difference between [the Biblical] universe and the modern one revealed by science is as the difference between a dust-flecked ray in a barn and the sublime arch of the Milky Way in the skies.[26]

Such a view is almost identical to that of Thomas Paine in <u>The Age of Reason</u>, the apologia for Deism. Clemens's writing his brother Orion on March 23, 1878, that

> Neither Howells nor I believe in hell or the divinity of the Savior, but no matter, the Savior is none the less a sacred Personage, and a man should have no desire or disposition to refer to him lightly, profanely, or otherwise than with the profoundest reverence.[27]

suggests a Boston Unitarian gentility in the treatment of a "sacred Personage," again a rationalistic approach to religion. Finally, during his walking tour of Europe in August-September,

1878 with his friend the Reverend Joe Twichell, Clemens "confessed": "Joe, . . . I don't believe in your religion at all." Clemens says that he has lived "a lie" whenever he pretended to believe. "Sometimes, I have been almost a believer, but it immediately drifts away . . . I don't believe one word of your Bible was inspired by God anymore than any other book. . . . from beginning to end--atonement and all," it is manmade. "The problem of life and death and eternity and the true conception of God is a bigger thing than is contained in that book."[28] The significant point here is in the final sentence of this confession: "The problem of life and death and eternity." Clemens recognized the problem, knew the conventional answers, rejected them, and was left on quest, as it were, to find his own solutions. He could probably have told Twichell not just that for a moment he had been almost a believer in a Christian solution, but a Deist solution, a Rousseauist solution, and any other that came his way. So by mid-career Samuel Clemens makes a clean breast of where he stands with relation to God, man, and the world. But instead of losing interest in matters spiritual after acknowledging his loss of faith, he makes evident in many ways an increasing concern with the social and political implications of the traditional Christian faith which he has theoretically disavowed.

He reveals a pragmatic religious spirit if not orthodoxy in his sketch of the backwoods villager Nicodemus Dodge, introduced casually in <u>A Tramp Abroad</u> when the author-tramp recalls "a loose-jointed, longlegged, jeans-clad, countrified cub of about sixteen [who] lounged in one day" to seek a job at the same Missouri printing office where Sam Clemens himself was employed. When the editor asks Nicodemus whether he belongs to a church, Nicodemus answers:

> "Well, boss, you've kind o' got me, thar--and yit you hain't got me so mighty much, nuther. I think if a feller he'ps another feller when he's in trouble, and don't cuss, and don't do no mean things, nur noth'n' he ain' no business to do, and don't spell the Saviour's name with a little g, he ain't runnin' no resks--he's about as saift as he b'long to a church."[29]

Twain portrays here a villager who, echoing his creator, has apparently rejected church dogma except the dread of its hereafter, but retained much of the ethical value of Christianity, which indeed is precisely what Deism did. Such a stance is reflective of Clemens's own written credo of the early 1880's.

Clemens begins formally with the one-sentence, one paragraph declaration, "I believe in God the Almighty" and proceeds to enumerate flagrantly anti-Christian, anti-Calvinist beliefs: that the Almighty has never had any direct communication with man, never "made Himself visible to mortal eyes at any time or in any place"; that the Bible is altogether man-made--"the Old and New Testaments were imagined and written by man, and no line in them was authorized by God."[30] Clemens further asserts that "the goodness, the justice, and the mercy of God are manifested in His works" and that these virtues "are manifested toward me in this life; the logical conclusion is that they will be manifested toward me in the life to come if there should be one. . . . There may be a hereafter, and there may not be. I am wholly indifferent about it." If there is, "I feel sure it will be for some more sane useful purpose than to flounder about for ages in a lake of fire and brimstone for having violated a confusion of ill-defined and contradictory rules said . . . to be of divine institution."[31] All of these comments are in the tradition of eighteenth century rationalism--a rejection of "divine intervention" or the supernatural, the mystical, an emphasis upon the "useful," the "sane," the "logical conclusion," "manifestations" in "this life," rejection of the "ill-defined" and "contradictory" rules. Applying logic and reason each step of the way, Twain can understand why the Almighty might "annihilate [man] when he shall have proved himself incapable of reaching perfection . . . but to roast him forever for the mere pleasure of seeing him roast would not be reasonable--even the atrocious God imagined by the Jews would tire of the spectacle eventually."[32] This is a most interesting sentence in charting Clemens's precise religious position. There is first of all the notion of eighteenth century's "perfectibility" of man which Clemens seems to accept only tentatively in speculating upon "when he shall have proved himself incapable."[33] The rationalists of the eighteenth century were more optimistic than this. But there is the rejection of damnation by "reason."

Again Clemens sounds much like an orthodox deist in saying, "I believe the universe is governed by strict and immutable laws"; by contrast, "the world's moral laws are the outcome of the world's experience. It needed no God to come down out of heaven to tell men that murder and theft and the other immoralities are bad, . . . "[34] By insisting that such laws are the result of experience rather than innate ideas, Clemens is adhering to a *tabula rasa* theory. Such a view is confusing in the light of his earlier opposition of the "good heart" against the "badly trained conscience." This inconsistency in turn suggests that in writing his *credo* Clemens might have been trying to be scientific--holding not so much to what he believed to be true, but to what he could see might be true based upon evidence. He had no evidence of the "good heart," which may be why he will a little later push the idea of an enlightened self-interest, which can come close to the idea of a "sound heart."

Clemens's next statement on the effects of religion is also revealing. "I am not able to believe one's religion can affect his hereafter one way or the other, no matter what that religion may be"[35] is more a statement about the possibility of a life after death than it is anything else. But Clemens's saying, "I would not interfere with anyone's religion . . ." because "it may be a great comfort to him in this life--hence it is a valuable possession to him"[36] again concerns itself with the comforts to be found in this world. Thus, religion may be useful, not necessarily destructive. Modern Protestants have made their own religion truly valuable to humanity, Clemens explains, "by selecting the humaner passages of the Bible, and teaching them to the world, whilst allowing those of a different sort to lie dormant." Such practices have "produced the highest and purest and best individuals which modern society has known."[37] It is fairly clear here that Clemens's animus was not so much against religion as it was against the institutions that controlled the religious spirit. His virulent attacks are upon the hypocrites who appropriate the language of religion to achieve an irreligious end. And the danger is always present in the book called the Bible, for though the "humaner passages" make it "the most valuable of books," the same Biblical authority for "all the religious atrocities of the Middle Ages is still in it," and it may again become "the heavy curse to the world as it was formerly."[38] Thus the Bible can be a source of good or a source of evil; what it becomes depends upon the tests its passages are subjected to. It is not a reliable instrument no matter whether it is the handiwork of men or divinely inspired because it is basically inconsistent. Thus,

> God could have said "Thou shalt not commit adultery;" but He would not have followed it up in the same book by plainly violating His own law with Mary the betrothed bride of Joseph.[39]

and

> Straight is the gate and narrow is the way, <u>few there be</u>," etc. . . . the utterance of the same authority which commands man to "multiply and replenish the earth."[40]

Clemens sees these last contradictory injunctions to "Meekly and obediently proceed to beget children, with the distinct understanding that <u>nearly all</u> of them must become fuel for the fires of hell." Anyone "who could obey such a command under such an understanding would be simply a monster . . ."⁴¹ However, he concludes, fortunately down in their hearts men do not believe such an affront to their reason. Thus, not only must scripture be submitted to tests of reason, it must also be submitted to tests of "feeling," and implicit here, I believe, is that all such moral injunctions must be submitted to such tests.

That Clemens tried to summarize the core of his religious belief is itself important, indicating either that he feels so keenly the loss of his original faith that he is driven to recover what has been lost, or indicating confusion as to what he did indeed believe--to write it down to understand it himself. In any case, he could see that though Calvinism had no answers, Deism too fell somewhat short, but for the most part, Clemens's statements of belief do precisely what Thomas Paine's did in <u>The Age of Reason</u>--attack orthodoxy and embrace an Enlightenment view of God and the universe. The belief that the Bible is not of divine origin but entirely the work of man, that the universe is governed by strict and immutable laws that by the use of its reason mankind can understand, and that the afterlife, if it exists, is less monstrous than the hell of everlasting fire and brimstone--such doctrines suggest that Clemens has moved toward a comprehension of a Supreme Force more kind and a mankind more worthy than Calvinism offered. But Clemens will continue his spiritual quest, torn between Calvinism and Deism, to fashion his own "more rational" deity, as well as his personal Bible. It would prove to be a difficult undertaking, for his own godhead would prove to be full of inconsistency, at first benign and later a malignant Force, just as his own Bible that he labels "a gospel of despair" will hold out both hope and its utter loss for humanity. Inconsistently, too, he will preach in terms more and more raucous his latter-day Calvinist doctrine of the damned human race, while at the same time in his satire he simultaneously voices a kind of religion of humanity to goad the society of the time--the same damned human race--to "reform itself upward."

By 1885 this duality is illustrated and clarified in several direct utterances of key doctrines in his later "gospel." "Happiness," Clemens told the Hartford Monday Evening Club on February 19, 1883, springs from satisfying the selfish impulses of one's heart. Every human action, good or bad, originates in the same way, and "if there are two desires in man's heart he has no choice between the two but must obey the strongest, there being no such thing as free will in the composition of any human being that ever lived."[42]

Such a statement can be construed to support the idea of innate ideas, if the desires are born with the heart, or the idea of a <u>tabula rasa</u> if the desires come from an external environment, but the denial of free-will, the return to predestination is a denial of perfectibility and Enlightenment principles.

To support this no-free-will concept--even as early as 1883-- Clemens fell back on a favorite metaphor. Man is a machine, no more and no less, without any claim to personal merit or demerit and thus, logically without any capacity whatever for improvement. Such a mix is extremely confusing. The idea of man as machine responding to an external environment and without claim to personal merit or demerit is certainly in keeping with the idea of a tabula rasa, but the incapacity to improve is once more quite Calvinistic, without Calvinism's emphasis upon demerit or depravity inborn.

But as Paine notes, in "What is Happiness?" Twain contradicts his own deterministic theory by suggesting a way for us not to gratify our selfish impulses but instead to steer them in the direction of human betterment:

> "Diligently train your ideals upward, and still upward, toward a summit where you will find your chiefest pleasure, in conduct which, while contenting you, will be sure to confer benefits upon your neighbor and the community."[43]

The only difference between this statement from the paper read in 1883 and its final restatement in What Is Man? is that the latter italicizes upward and still upward and has a comma after pleasure, details which emphasize the author's contradictory reasoning, though they might result from the accidents of printing. The significant point is that by the time he makes this observation in What Is Man?, Twain has already admitted that despite "there being no such thing as free will in the composition of any human being that ever lived" man is urged to train his "ideals upward" "to confer benefits upon . . . neighbor and community." "Man is never anything but what his outside influences have made him," Twain claims, and these outside influences "train him downward or they train him upward . . . He has only to change his habitat--his <u>associations</u>" to alter his prospects. And while "the impulse to do it must come only from the outside," the changed habitat or associations may furnish "<u>Initiatory Impulses toward high ideas</u>" that could start him "upward" toward a new life. Indeed the admonition quoted above is specifically set forth as a "plan for the betterment of the race's condition, . . . [taught by] All the great religions--"[44] Several points may be made here, one of which is that Twain can be caught up in the same sort of contradiction implicit in any predestinarian concept--why, if fate is already pre-destined, bother to urge man to change his ways; man cannot finally help himself. Another point may be that Twain is not being contradictory so much as he is advocating a Skinnerian approach to human behavior, that he is indeed a behaviorist. If the training is thorough, there will be no deviation from it; the trick is simply to train toward the "good" rather than toward the bad. But whatever the interpretation, there is no question that Twain is finally contradictory--either the race is perfectible or it is not, regardless of why or the means of achieving perfectibility. Thus Paine quite rightly says that Clemens was never more than a pessimist in theory at any time."[45]

Still further utterances from the period raise further questions on what has seemed to be Clemens's Enlightenment attitudes at this time in his life. In a letter to Howells

January 7, 1884, he wrote about a book he had begun to write:

> Its hidden motive will illustrate a but-little considered fact in human nature; that the religion you are born in you _die_ in, no matter what apparently reasonabler religious folly may seem to have taken its place meanwhile & abolished & obliterated it.[46]

If this message is to be taken as anything more than a passing thought, Clemens is saying that he is to die a Presbyterian, or, if he did indeed absorb the doctrines of Deism from his father and from his uncle John Quarles, a Presbyterian-Deist. And the implicit contradiction of no-free-will and perfectibility may be either his own Presbyterianism as it was practiced--preach the predestination but live perfectibility--or a true combination of these two childhood influences.

But Clemens's comment to Howells is modified somewhat in What Is Man? when he observes that ". . . as soon as the Seeker finds what he is thoroughly convinced is the truth, he" stops seeking and "gives the rest of his days to hunting junk to patch it and caulk it and . . . make it weather-proof and keep it from caving in on him." True Presbyterians remain Presbyterian, Mohammedans, Mohammedan, and should "a humble, earnest, and sincere Seeker after Truth" find "the proposition that the moon is made of green cheese nothing could ever budge him from that position; for he is nothing but an automatic machine, and must obey the laws of his construction."[47] At least in this passage Twain allows someone to find what he is thoroughly convinced is the truth before becoming fixed in his belief, something sometimes different from being born into a religion.

To be sure, Clemens's no-belief in the old dogma did not mean nihilism, as some Twainians have proclaimed. It is certainly not "the ultimate negation" which critics from Howells or Brooks on down to Justin Kaplan or Professor Frederick attribute to him. Clemens rages against the world primarily because he is frustrated as he seeks the meaning of existence in a quest for a viable faith.

In a letter dated June 1, 1885--six months after publication of <u>Huckleberry Finn</u>, Clemens shows that the pendulum has swung to outright denial, the profession of unbelief. The letter to Charles Warren Stoddard, an amiable, unworldly friend of Clemens's San Francisco days, is Clemens's answer to Stoddard's spiritual autobiography entitled <u>A Troubled Heart</u> that described in detail the author's conversion to Roman Catholicism: My dear Charley--I have read it. Yes, I think you were right to print it: for . . . all sorts of people . . . require all sorts of comforting; consequently" some require the comfort found in religion. "Peace of mind is a most valuable thing. The Bible has robbed the majority of the world of it during many centuries; it is fair that in return it should give some to an individual here & there. But "one must not suppose that "absolute peace of mind is obtainable only through some form [of] religious belief; no, on the contrary, I have found that as perfect peace is to be found in absolute unbelief. I look back with the same shuddering horror upon . . . when I believed, as you do . . . when you were afraid you did not believe." Since both are certain now and there is rest in certainty, "let us be content. May your belief & my unbelief never more be shaken in this life! You have told your story eloquently, beautifully,--how well a gifted man *can* argue from false premises, false history, false everything!"⁴⁸ Seymour Gross observes that the letter

> . . . affords further evidence of how much Twain's inner life was shaped by the need to escape the "shuddering horror" of his Calvinistic upbringing with "its legacy (which Twain never shook off) of "a Presbyterian conscience [that] knew but the one duty--to hunt and harry its slave upon all pretexts and occasions . . ."⁴⁹

Gross adds, quite rightly, that Samuel Clemens's latter-day bitterness illustrates the strains of this very same burdensome legacy, specifically the unbelief and "simplistic determinism" of *What Is Man*? But Gross sees no contradiction, for instance, between Clemens's indictment of the Catholic Church as essentially false and his enthusiastic approval of it some years later, after his daughter Jean enters a convent when Clemens writes his wife: "And away deep down in my heart, I feel that if they make a good strong unshakable Catholic of her I shan't be the least bit sorry. It is doubtless the most peaceful and restful of all religions. If I had it I would not trade it for anything on earth."⁵⁰ Thus, the vaunted "perfect . . . peace . . . [from] absolute unbelief" which Clemens claims to have attained simply cannot be taken at face value, because for the next twenty-five years he doggedly indicts Calvinism and its legacy of a tyrannical Jehovah. Indeed, about the time Clemens announces his new-found spiritual solace to Stoddard, his inner turmoil manifests itself in an essay titled "The Character of Man" (1885) published in Paine's edition of <u>Mark Twain's Autobiography</u>. In "The Character of Man" the abstract thinker launches what must rank as his angriest, more contemptuous indictment of man in Twain's career at that time.[51] Apparently what galled him into the diatribe was the recent "contemptible behavior" he had witnessed among Hartford Republicans who professed to admire independence of thought and action and honesty in expressing one's opinions, yet who voted for "the disreputable candidate" on the Republican ticket, James G. Blaine. Rereading "The Character of Man" on January 11, 1906, Clemens remarked, "It was long ago, but it plainly means Blaine." For Clemens, the vote for Blaine is a perfect illustration of "the sweet-smelling sugar-coated lies" that men conspire to perpetuate, both the "trunk-lie" that among them there is independence of thought and action, and the "branch-lie" that "not all men are slaves." Another branch lie is "that conscience, man's moral medicine chest, is not only created by the Creator, but is put into man ready-charged with the right and only true and authentic correctives of conduct--" Still another branch lie: "that we are . . . individuals, and have natures of our own, instead of being the tail-end of a tape-worm eternity of ancestors with this so called individuality of ours a decayed and rancid mush of inherited instincts, and teachings derived, atom by atom, stench by stench, from the entire line of that sorry column, and not so much of original matter in it as you could balance on a needle point and examine under a microscope." Man was not made for any useful purpose, and indeed "his working himself up out of the oyster bed was probably matter of surprise and regret to the Creator." Whatever "noble qualities" he may display--gentleness, amiability, courage, etc.--"other animals share . . . with him," but with the difference that they are "free from the blacknesses and rottennesses of his character." And thus Twain proceeds to his foregone conclusion reached two years before in "What Is Happiness?":

> Let us skip the other lies, for brevity's sake . . . man is what he is--loving, toward his own, . . . his family, his friends--and otherwise the buzzing, busy, trivial, enemy of his race--who tarries his little day, does his little dirt, commends himself to God, and then goes out into the darkness, to return no more . . . selfish even in death.[52]

As in "What Is Happiness?" out of one side of his mouth he talks like a determinist who recognizes mankind as "the tail-end of a tapeworm eternity of ancestors . . . a decayed and rancid mush of inherited instincts and teachings" but out of the other side, he sounds like the moralist who will not exempt his fellows from blame or from their individual moral responsibility. Calvinism has reared its head in the insistence upon "inherited instincts," and Rationalism must take its lumps in "rancid mush of . . . teachings" that eventually become a matter of "regret to the Creator."

"The Character of Man" follows shortly after the publication of <u>Huckleberry Finn</u>, Twain's most powerfully affirmative work, and thus encourages a view of the later Clemens as a man led by scientific determinism and ultimate despair. There is little doubt that Clemens experienced such trains of thought and such feelings, but evidence reveals they were neither lasting nor even self-consistent at the time of their expression. The inconsistency reveals that his quest for answers was not completed in the years ahead.

ENDNOTES TO CHAPTER V

1. DeVoto, <u>Mark Twain's America</u>, p. 304.
2. Geismar, <u>Mark Twain: American Prophet</u> (Boston: Houghton Mifflin, 1970), p. 47.
3. Smith, <u>Mark Twain: The Development of a Writer</u>, pp. 88, 89.
4. Blair, p. 86.
5. <u>Tom Sawyer</u>, p. 44.
6. <u>Tom Sawyer</u>, p. 3.
7. <u>Tom Sawyer</u>, p. 34.
8. <u>Tom Sawyer</u>, pp. 54-55.
9. <u>Tom Sawyer</u>, p. 47.
10. <u>Tom Sawyer</u>, p. 57.
11. Geismar, p. 47.
12. <u>Tom Sawyer</u>, Ch. X, pp. 95-96.
13. <u>Tom Sawyer</u>, p. 82.
14. Author's National Edition, 25 Vols. (New York: Harper, 1907-18), Vol. II, pp. 302-325 (p. 308).
15. <u>Carnival of Crime</u>, pp. 316-17.
16. <u>Carnival of Crime</u>, p. 325.
17. <u>Mark Twain and Southwestern Humor</u>, p. 203.
18. Geismar, pp. 4, 5, 54.
19. "Recent Carnival of Crime," p. 325.
20. Blair, <u>Mark Twain & Huck Finn</u>, p. 143.
21. Author's National Edition, 25 Vols., II, pp. 252-54.
22. <u>Some Rambling Notes</u>, pp. 263-67.

23. Some Rambling Notes, pp. 343-59.
24. Budd, Mark Twain Social Philosopher, p. 64.
25. Blair, p. 184.
26. Paine, I, p. 412.
27. Letters, I, p. 323.
28. Paine, II, p. 631.
29. A Tramp Abroad, Author's National Edition, Vol. III, Ch. XXIII, p. 206.
30. See What Is Man? and Other Philosophical Writings, ed. Paul Baender, The Works of Mark Twain, Vol. 19 (Berkeley: University of California Press, 1973), pp. 56-59 (p. 56).
31. What Is Man?, pp. 56-57.
32. What Is Man?, pp. 56-57.
33. What Is Man?, p. 56.
34. What Is Man?, p. 57.
35. What Is Man?, p. 57.
36. What Is Man?, p. 57.
37. What Is Man?, pp. 57-58.
38. What Is Man?, p. 58.
39. What Is Man?, p. 58.
40. What Is Man?, p. 58.
41. What Is Man?, pp. 58-59.
42. Mark Twain in Eruption, p. 239.
43. Paine, II, p. 744.
44. What Is Man?, pp. 47, 54, 55.
45. Paine, II, p. 744.

46. *Mark Twain-Howells Letters*, II, p. 461.
47. *What Is Man*?, pp. 74-75.
48. Seymour, L. Gross, "Mark Twain on the Serenity of Unbelief," *Huntington Library Quarterly*, XXII (22), (May 1959), pp. 260-62 (pp. 261-62).
49. *Gross*, p. 262.
50. *Gross*, p. 262.
51. *What Is Man?* pp. 60-64 (p. 60).
52. *What Is Man*?, pp. 60-64.

CHAPTER VI: HUCKLEBERRY FINN

Up to the writing of <u>Huckleberry Finn</u> Samuel Clemens had been exposed to four evident and contrary, if not contradictory, "philosophies," four sometimes conflicting attitudes toward man and god and the nature of the universe. Calvinism portrays man as innately evil and finally powerless to help himself; god is all benevolent in spite of this and the universe created by god is hostile to man. Deism portrays man in Enlightenment terms as born neither good nor evil (<u>tabula rasa</u>), capable of either according to the "reason" exercised by man and endowed by god; evil is simply a departure from "reason"; God is rational and the universe works according to God's reasoned laws. Romanticism portrays man as innately good, corrupted by the unnatural or social; god is good and the universe is sympathetic to that innate goodness. The scientific determinism that Clemens absorbed is, in some respect, a combination of Enlightenment and Calvinist views. Such a view has man born neither good nor evil because the terms "good" and "evil" have no real meaning. Man is, however, powerless, subject to laws of nature that he does not understand. In its acceptance of man's powerlessness, scientific determinism is much like Calvinism. In its acknowledgement of man's being subject to universal laws of nature, scientific determinism is much like the Enlightenment conception of the universe. What is missing from the scientific deterministic view is the idea of good and evil, the idea of "god" as good. Thus scientific determinism attempts to avoid a moral stance or it presupposes a moral stance independent of god and accepts a short-term amoral view of life. However, if man can ever understand the "laws" governing his behavior, he will no longer be powerless and will then be in a position to adjust or adapt in some way to those laws and perhaps "create" a moral world. This, it seems, must be implicit in any "deterministic" view of the world--why else bother to explain to the world that it has no choice but is simply victimized by uncontrollable forces. In the long run, however, once those laws are known, man will have choices; at that point he will be held accountable if not to god then to man himself. The alternative to such a line of reasoning is that the "telling" the world it is being victimized is not a conscious act; it is not a message of hopelessness to the world but a cry of pain and anguish with no message. It is expression, not communication. Samuel Clemens may have written in pain and anguish, but most of the time he was communicating, not merely expressing, and the last of these four "attitudes" available to Twain, in large part explains the myth of his despair in the confusion of attitudes that make up the significant art of Huckleberry Finn. This masterpiece, like Whitman's "Song of Myself," contains the seeds of all Clemens's religious thought and speculation.

DeVoto long ago pointed out a balancing of positive and negative forces and attitudes in Huckleberry Finn. There is,

DeVoto says, "detachment . . . but it is still somehow compassionate; condemnation" is complete but "somehow magnanimous. The damned human race is displayed with derision and abhorrence, yet this is on the ground that it has fallen short of its own decencies." There is "a vindication not only of freedom, but of loyalty and decency, kindness and courage; and it is of the essence of Mark Twain that this vindication is made by means of a boy who is a spokesman of the folk mind and whom experience has taught wariness and skepticism."[1] "Detachment," "affirmation," "compassionate," "condemnation," "abhorrence," and "damned." These are all important words in an understanding of Twain's position in the novel. The kind of balancing described is nothing new in criticism of the novel; there is the familiar division of the "good," the "primitive," the "river," versus the "bad," the "civilized," the "shore." The novel, even so, is yet much more complicated and realistic than such simple divisions indicate, and the complication is a consequence of Clemens's own confusion about where he stood in his perception of the world.

In *Huckleberry Finn*, what unfolds on the one hand is a vision of an unredeemed society whose leading citizens do lip service to the evangelical, crusading Protestantism of the day, while they, mostly either rascals or fools, practice a shabby morality. The society seems to be contaminated to its roots by a sham Christianity which we see through the eyes of the narrator protagonist. Unlike its Edenic portrayal in *Tom Sawyer*, St. Petersburg now shares something of the universal damnation, except for Huck and Jim who flee the village as if it were unholy. Huck is escaping from the lowest as well as its highest social strata--from the bestiality of a drunken "nigger-hater" father and the suffocatingly proper guardians of virtue, the Widow Douglas and her vinegarish old maid sister, Miss Watson, the voice of evangelical Protestism. Huck's fellow fugitive, Nigger Jim, literally <u>belongs</u> to the same citadel of respectability. To devout Christians like Widow Douglas and Miss Watson--and indeed to Huck himself--Jim is not human; he is an expensive animal. According to H. N. Smith, a decade after the novel appeared Sam Clemens recorded in notes about his native village: "The whole community was agreed as to one thing--the awful sacredness of slave property."[2] Here was the gospel truth adhered to not just by slave owners but by "the paupers, the loafers, the tag-rag & the bob-tail of the community, & in a passionate and uncompromising form . . ." for, as Clemens also noted, "the conscience--that unerring monitor--can be trained to approve any wild thing you want it to approve if you begin its education early and stick to it."[3] "Any wild thing" would embrace the two essentials of Huck's education--Calvinism's terrifying after-life for the mass of mankind and its championship of slavery. Such an explanation looks forward to the indictment of the race as cowardly in "The Character of Man" written in the mid-eighties, as well as to the determinism of <u>What Is Man</u>? two decades later. It also attributes to conscience the all-powerful force behind human behavior which Clemens identifies as and equates with Public Opinion in these early and late attempts to articulate his gospel. To Clemens, mankind is the slave of both forces, which are at bottom one and the same thing, since conscience and public opinion are twin aspects of what he would call "the Master Passion--the hunger for Self-Approval."[4] In any case, St. Petersburg believed that slavery was part of the divine plan, and young Huck viscerally absorbed this belief, and Huck and Jim flee the town to journey down river and encounter varied types of the species Man and reflect Clemens's equally varied attitudes toward the species. There is a succession of rogues, feuding aristocrats, would-be lynchers, murderers, and god-crazy revivalists. Against such a degenerate society, the two fugitives shine forth as beacons of hope and goodness in a lost world.

One of the most persistent of the social pressures experienced by Huck is that of "conscience," which comes to him through two somewhat contrasting views by the Widow Douglas and Miss Watson. Branch argues cogently that in the Widow Douglas's household, Huck learns two quite different providences: the hell-fire-and-damnation Jehovah of Miss Watson's Calvinism, and the more kindly Almighty of the Widow. Miss Watson would have Huck stick to the straight-and-narrow for his own safety and thus avoid "the bad place"; whereas the Widow urges him above all to do right by others and thus attain "the good place"-- she "would talk about Providence in a way to make a body's mouth water."[5] Confused by what Branch describes as a conflict between "self-centered, conventional morality and humanitarian idealism,"[6] Huck finally decides with a mixture of pragmatism and humility, to follow the Providence of the Widow simply because he felt he had a better "show" with it than with the other:

> I thought it all out, and reckoned I would belong to the Widow's if he wanted me, though I couldn't make out how he was a-going to be any better off than what he was before, seeing I was so ignorant, and so kind of low-down and ornery.[7]

Though Branch does not note it, the difference between the providences of the Widow and Miss Watson is the difference between Calvinism and Deism. Calvinism emphasizes avoidance of evil; Deism emphasizes the commitment to engage in good. Avoiding the bad is essentially selfish--keeping oneself from the fires of hell. Pursing the good helps others, is altruistic. Huck's self-assessment in the passage quoted above is that of an unregenerate Calvinist, "ignorant, and so kind of low-down and ornery." This is obviously a self-image imposed by convention, by his community.

Certainly the Calvinist view of man dominates much of the novel. There is instance after instance of depravity, though it is rarely clear that the depravity is innate. There is an Enlightenment view of man that shows how the "conscience" can be trained "upward" to achieve good for one's neighbors. Finally, Huck and Jim appear to be Romantic incarnations of innate goodness following the dictates of "heart" rather than conscience or reason. As Huck moves through the novel, his actions and sometimes his thoughts reflect his reactions to these alternative views. In large part, Huck's spiritual or moral growth is dependent upon his choice of the options offered him by the conflicting philosophies of the Widow and Miss Watson, a conflict manifested at several points in the novel between the heart and the twisted conscience.

When Huck and Jim near Cairo and Jim announces his plan to save the money to buy his family from slavery and "if their master wouldn't sell them they'd get an Ab'litionist to go and steal them," Huck is horrified: "It almost froze me to hear such talk," he declares. Jim's resolve flouts everything Huck has learned from Pap Finn and from the Widow's Christian home. This twisted social conscience at first makes him decide to turn Jim in and Huck rows to shore to do just that--abide by the dictates of conscience; but when he tries to tell the planters, who appear hunting for "the five niggers that run off tonight," that his man on the raft is black, "the words wouldn't come . . . I warn't man enough--hadn't the spunk of a rabbit."[8] Such an encounter with his conscience supports several possibilities. Twain clearly means for Huck to follow his heart--thus the idea of an innate goodness. He also means to show the influence of social conditioning, which does not necessarily argue for a <u>tabula rasa</u>, but does indicate that what we choose to do is powerfully influenced by what we have been taught to do. In this particular instance, Huck has been taught wrong. It is ironic that he sees the cause of his choice without recognizing the rightness of it when he rationalizes his wicked ways: ". . . a body that don't get started right when he's little ain't got no show . . ." Huck is saying that if he is to make the right choice, society must teach him to make that choice, that choice is dependent upon environment. He believes that he lacked proper environment and thus cannot make the right choice. Irony would have us believe that Huck had the proper environment to make the choice to turn Jim in--it is, after all, everything taught him by Pap and everything else he has known in all of civilization. There is no indication he has ever seen an abolitionist; he knows only that they are bad. What more could environment do?

But in another sense, Twain can be arguing the nature-nurture point, that decisions are made by environmental influences perhaps most of the time, but that something else may come into play in such decisions. This does not mean that environmental influences have no effect, but that they are only partial. Something in Huck--Twain calls it "heart" --opposes environmental conditioning. That something would not necessarily come into play if environmental condition were not faulty to begin with, if it did not run counter to "nature."

But Huck does not let the issue stand here; he reasons further to the conclusion that his conscience would have stung him if he had told on Jim. "I'd feel bad," he says; "I'd feel just the same way I do now." He then concludes,

> Well, then, says I, what's the use you learning to do right when it's troublesome to do right and ain't no trouble to do wrong, and the wages is just the same? I was stuck. I couldn't answer that. So I reckoned I wouldn't bother no more about it, but after this always do whichever comes handiest at the time.[9]

If conscience is going to hurt him regardless of the choice he makes, then society has given him contradictory laws to uphold. This may be the case with Huck. Certainly his society has not taught him to help a slave go free, but it may well have taught him not to betray a decent human being. That society does not consider Jim human would be irrelevant if Huck considers him human. Another possibility is that Huck is mistakenly calling something "conscience" that is not conscience at all, but something called "heart," innate decency. To violate that decency would bring guilt, the same consequence to violating conscience.

So Huck resolves his problem pragmatically. If "the wages is the same," that is the results are the same regardless of the rightness or wrongness of an act, then it would indeed make sense to do the "handiest" or least inconvenient thing. The question of course is, are the wages the same? They are the same for Huck, but they are not the same for Jim. And it is doubtful if Huck would do the "handiest" thing if it meant that Jim must suffer, even when Huck's wages are the same. What Huck is disposing of here is the question of whether "learning" to do right is of any "use." He refuses to bother with this question any longer, much as Benjamin Franklin said of his conversion from free thinking, "though it might be true, it was not very useful," and so he became a Deist.

Huck has reached the same verdict expressed by the narrator in "Facts Concerning the Recent Carnival of Crime in Connecticut"

(1876): "It don't make no difference," Huck says, "whether you do right or wrong, a person's conscience ain't got no sense, and just goes for him anyway."[10] Huck is not far from Twain's gospel in What Is Man? (1898, 1906) in which the Old Man observes to the Young Man that a person can so train his ideals upward as to "content himself and confer benefits upon his neighbors and his community. Huck's moral decisions content Huck and help Jim," as Blair points out.[11]

Branch claims Huck's inner debate leads him finally to act with "instinctive rightness," which Huck himself condemns. Clemens acknowledges the triumph of Huck's virtue in a notebook entry he wrote for a lecture tour in 1895.[12] His plan for the lecture series, as the notebook shows, was to "get up an elaborate and formal lay sermon on morals and the conduct of life" to be illustrated by the lecture. He would, he said, support "the proposition that in a crucial moral emergency a sound heart is a safer guide than an ill-trained conscience . . . with a chapter from a book of mine where a sound heart and a deformed conscience come into collision and conscience suffers defeat. Two persons figure in the chapter: Jim, a middle-aged slave, and Huck Finn, a boy of 14." In those times, Twain says, "the whole community" agreed on "the awful sacredness of slave property. To help steal a horse or a cow was a low crime, but to help a hunted slave . . . or hesitate to promptly betray him to a slave-catcher when opportunity offered was a much baser crime, and carried with it a stain, a moral smirch which nothing could wipe away."[13] Clemens then says that paupers like Huck and "his worthless father" share this sentiment "in a passionate and uncompromising form" just as much as do slave-owners themselves. This fact, he says,

> . . . shows that strange thing, the conscience--the unerring monster--can be trained to approve any wild thing you <u>want</u> to approve if you begin its education early and stick to it.[14]

But Clemens raises an interesting question of interpretation here. If "conscience" approves, and conscience does approve Huck's betraying Jim--Huck feels good about his conscience later when he decides to do this--what is it that will not let him alone? Twain would have us to see that it is a "sound heart." Huck says that what won't let you alone is conscience too--"whether you do right or wrong, a person's conscience . . . just goes for him <u>anyway</u>." So Huck is calling his "sound Heart," Branch's "instinctive rightness," by the name of "conscience." Perhaps Twain is arguing that "if you begin its education early and stick to it" you will have the conscience supercede the sound heart.

Huck himself is not sophisticated enough to be aware of having engaged in a collision between a deformed conscience and a sound heart in which conscience suffers defeat. He only knows he has violated his society's central taboo. His unique background--from the tanyard at one level to the big-house-on-the-hill, the peak of Christian respectability at the other--binds him to the community values as the only ones he can imagine. For Huck the divine justice of slavery is part of his psyche not only because it has been breathed into him by his racist father, but also because it has been reinforced by his religious teachers, the Widow and Miss Watson. Pap Finn's son, in short, is "involved in civilization up to his ears," even though he is running away from it.[15]

By Huck's picture of the Grangerford household--its flaunting of the bible, the sickly sweet pictures, the unconsciously grotesque verse about death--Twain portrays another part of a perverted society, the Southern aristocracy, whose love of unreality becomes most evident in church. Both Grangerfords and Shepherdsons keep their guns between their knees or stand them against the wall of the church while Huck comments on the minister's sermon:

> It was pretty ornery preaching--all about brotherly-love . . .; but everybody said it was a good sermon, and they all talked it over going home, and had such a powerful lot to say about faith and good works and free grace and preforeordestination, and I don't know what all, that it did seem to be one of the roughest Sundays I had ever run across yet.[16]

Huck records without comment the Bible-reading, gun-totin' feuders going to church armed as for battle and listening intently to a sermon on brotherly love, the heart of the gospel of Christianity.

The Grangerford episode gives Huck yet another opportunity to hear the tenets of Calvinism in the Presbyterian church--"preforeordestination" and "free grace"--and to see the results of stupid pride. In Huck's and Jim's adventures with the King and the Duke, Twain widens his scope for the ridicule of Bible-belt religion in particular and the damned human race generally. The King and the Duke instigate a series of depredations with riverfolk that illuminate further the sham religion in the region; it is as though Twain is saying you have seen the bloodlust of a Southern aristocracy in the Grangerford's practice of high-toned Presbyterianism; now let me show you fundamentalist peasantry. The King makes no secret of his talent for bilking religious yokels. "Preachin's my line," he informs the Duke, "and workin' camp-meetin's missionaryin' around."[17] In Pokeville, the King and Huck find a crowd at the camp-meeting as immense as the unprecedented gathering during Sam Clemens's days as cub-printer when the famous revivalist Alexander Campbell brought his crusade to Hannibal.[18] To hear Huck tell it, "a thousand people [were] there from twenty mile around. The woods was full of teams and wagons . . ."[19] There was also preaching everywhere, under sheds made of poles covered with tree branches. Huck finds the singing "grand to hear," and when the revivalist "lines out" two more hymns for them to sing, the congregation burst into a frenzy. They "sung louder and louder, and . . . some begun to groan, and some begun to shout"; "the preacher begun to preach . . . in earnest" now, and started weaving about the platform "shouting out his words with all his might . . ." He finally holds his Bible above the furor and screams, "It's the brazen serpent in the wilderness! Look upon it and live!'"[20] And the people get the message. They begin screaming, "Glory!-- A-a-men!"

>   Oh, come to the mourner's bench! come, black with sin! (<u>amen</u>!) come sick and sore! (<u>amen</u>) come, pore and needy, sink in shame! (<u>a-a-men</u>!) come, . . . in your rags and sin and dirt! the waters that cleanse is free, the door of heaven stands open--oh, enter in and be at rest! (<u>a-amen</u>!) glory, glory hallelujah![21]

In the wild commotion, the throng struggled to get to the mourner's bench. "With tears streaming down their faces," Huck says, "they sung and shouted and flung themselves down on the straw, just crazy and wild."[22] What the preacher said could be heard no more.

The hysteria gives the King his cue to start "missionaryin'"; ". . . the first thing I knowed the King got-agoing, and you could hear him above everybody . . . next he went a-charging upon the platform and the preacher begged him to speak to the people, and he done it."[23] And the King walks away with eighty-seven dollars and seventy-five cents, "spiritual" kisses from young women in the crowd, and steals a three gallon jug of moonshine on his way out. In his treatment of the gullibility of these Pokeville villagers Twain is simply returning to a theme in <u>The Gilded Age</u> when Dilworthy's constituents allow his Bible-talking piety to overcome the obvious evidence of his corruption.

Still another element of society is found farther down the river in a town where down-at-the-heels, poor whites whittle until interrupted, "chawing tobacco, . . . gaping and yawning and stretching." Their idea of fun is to sick a dog on a sow which has "whalloped" herself down in the muddy street, and "laugh and look grateful for the noise." Even more fun is a dog fight or "putting turpentine on a stray dog and setting fire to him, or tying a tin pan to his tail and see him run himself to death."[24] The implication is that this is what the camp-meeting people are like when they are not being religious. Totally insensitive to human feelings and impervious to decent behavior or human tragedy, they have the raw curiosity of not very bright children--their highest form of entertainment is mime and evidently everyone carries his personal "bottle" about with him. Twain is unrelenting in his portrayal of these people and has Colonel Sherburn accurately assess them in a speech to the crowd on the courage of the common man: "'The average man's a coward . . . The pitifulest thing out is a mob.'"[25] That the mob does as Sherburn commands, substantiates his point--the average man is a coward. And as for the un-average man--the aristocrats like Sherburn, the Grangerfords, the Shepherdsons--he is senselessly brutal and cruel. Added up, Twain's gallery of characters is so generally depraved, there don't seem to be enough left to worry about. And all are religious.

Even farther down the river, the King and the Duke rely again on false piety and sentiment to defraud the Wilks girls of their inheritance. Posing as brothers of the dead Peter Wilks, the King and the Duke burst into a crying binge that Huck says "was enough to make a body ashamed of the human race."[26] The King is early opposed by a single voice of reason in a Dr. Robinson, friend of the deceased, who pronounces the King "the thinnest kind of imposter."[27] Robinson's rationality is no more effective than the rational opposition to Senator Dilworthy in

The Gilded Age: the people *will* be deceived by their emotions. And yet it is Huck's "heart," the emotions, that resists his malformed conscience and causes him to make the good choice. Twain, then, is not castigating feeling, but either false feeling--that evinced by the Kind--or feeling unattended by reason that makes people incapable of distinguishing truth from falsity. Robinson may well be one whose mind has been "trained upward" not just in the matter of conscience, but in the matter of discerning reality.

Subsequent developments in the swindle of the Wilks sisters reveal that Huck has not held to his resolve to "do whichever comes handiest at the time" when the "wages" of doing right and wrong "is just the same." It is certainly not "handy" for him to steal the Wilks sisters's money from the King and the Duke or to hide it in the coffin, which Huck comes to see when he thinks on what he has done:

> So, says I, s'pose somebody has hogged that bag on the sly? now how do I know whether to write Mary Jane or not? S'pose she dug him up and didn't find nothing, what would she think of me? Blame it, I says, I might get hunted up and jailed. . . . I wish to goodness I'd just let it alone, dad fetch the whole business![28]

Huck keeps himself in a stew by pursuing Widow Douglas's Providence as he goes out of his way to do his bit for others. His ignoring the consequences before he acts is evidence not simply of heroism, but of innate goodness as well. He lands himself in further trouble by reassuring Mary Jane and impulsively blurting out the truth; as he says, "Laws, it was out before I could think!"

Though he will later feel good about what he has done--"I felt very good . . . I judged I had done it neat" this does not alter his conception of himself in Calvinistic terms. When Mary Jane in her gratitude says she will pray for him, Huck observes to himself, "Pray for me! . . . I reckon if she knowed me she'd take a job that was more nearer her size."[29]

The King and the Duke having lost all in the Wilks scheme are reduced to selling Jim into slavery. Huck's dismay--he cries genuinely for only the second time in the novel--is followed by his famous moral dilemma and his resolution. He begins by rationalizing. He recalls from their talks on the river how family-conscious Jim is and reflects that Jim would be much better off back with his wife and children "as long as he's got to be slave."[30] This, he sees, will not work: Miss Watson would be so disgusted by his "rascality and ungratefulness for leaving her," she'd sell him down the river for sure; and if she didn't do that, "everybody despises an ungrateful nigger and would make Jim feel ornery and disgraced."[31] What happens to Jim becomes Huck's chief concern--he will be "sold down the river" or he will "feel ornery and disgraced." Finally, it comes down to what Jim will <u>feel</u>, and he must not feel "disgrace." One is reminded of McCaslin Edmonds' telling young Isaac in "The Old People" that there is only one thing worse than death and that is shame.

In opposition to what Jim will feel is what society will think, so there is the opposition perhaps of not just individual versus society but of thought and feeling. The opposition extends beyond the moral and into the religious when Huck finally decides to "go to hell." Here he unequivocally equates the voice of society with divine truth and goodness. "I do not think the voice I hear is from the devil," Emerson wrote, "but if it is, then I must be the devil's child." Such unqualified individualism, such defiance is the equivalent of Ahab's, the archetypal radical romantic defying the gods, Prometheus bearing the forbidden gift of fire to man.

Amidst the agony with his conscience, Huck lapses into insincerity, specifically "the chiding voice" of Miss Watson's evangelical Protestantism: ". . . all of a sudden . . . here was the plain hand of Providence slapping me in the face and letting me know my wickedness was being watched all the time from up there in heaven. . ."[32]

Huck next tries to allay his fears of Miss Watson's awesome Deity always threatening him, when he rationalizes in the vernacular, that "I was brung up wicked, and so I warn't so much to blame."[33] But such rationalization won't wash, because he hears another rasping voice inside him, like Miss Watson herself and in her very accent:

> There was the Sunday-school, you could 'a' gone to it; and if you'd 'a' done it they'd 'a' learn't you there that people that acts as I'd been acting about that nigger goes to everlasting fire.[34]

The very thought of eternal fire and brimstone, the Calvinist doctrine of St. Petersburg fixed in his mind makes Huck shiver so that he decides to try Miss Watson's advice on how to avoid it:

he will pray to be a better boy. But the words won't come. "It warn't no use to try to hide it from Him," he says. "I knowed very well why they wouldn't. It was because my heart wasn't right; . . . it was because I was playing double . . . <u>letting on</u> to give up sin, but . . . holding onto the biggest one of all," pretending to "do the right thing and the clean thing, and . . . write that nigger's owner and tell her where he was; but deep in me I knowed it was a lie, and He knowed it."[35] His heart isn't <u>right</u>, a requisite for prayer, and Huck knows that he has no real intention of writing. The heart must be resolved, and so he sits down and writes Miss Watson and at once feels "light as a feather . . . all washed cleaned of sin for the first time I ever felt so in my life, and I knowed I could pray now."[36]

So Huck reasons through to a conclusion. It is wicked to steal property and wickedness will bring you to hell. It is right and just to return stolen property and rightness will get you to heaven. But the reasoning leaves something to be desired and the flaws in the reasoning are brought about when Huck remembers not the absolute laws of his society, his conscience, Calvinism, but the particular concrete experiences he has shared with Jim: "I see Jim before me all the time," he muses--in the daytime and at night, "sometimes moonlight, sometime storms, and we a-floating along, talking and singing and laughing."[37] "I see him standing my watch on top of his'n, 'stead of calling me, so I could go on sleeping; and see . . . how glad he was when I come back out of the fog; and when I come to him again in the swamp, up there where the feud was; . . ."[38] And so he takes up the letter in his hand: "I was a-trembling, because I'd got to decide, forever, betwixt two things, and I knowed it." His choice is between society and "conscience" and humanity and "heart."[39] And Huck decides, "'All right then I'll <u>go</u> to hell.'" Huck's feeling clearly dominates what his reason tells him and he makes the choice any romantic would approve.

Samuel Clemens interpreted Huck's preliminary bout with his Inner Master quite specifically as showing that "in a crucial moral emergency a sound heart is a safer guide than an ill-trained conscience."[40] Huck's conscience has been acquired from his guttersnipe father, from the Widow Douglas and her dour Calvinistic sister, and from his close association with Jim and whatever else in the way of society St. Petersburg has provided him over the years. The values he has absorbed are the reality of a wrathful Jehovah and the sacredness of slavery as an institution. Upon both grounds his conscience requires Huck on pain of roasting in hell forever to return the runaway slave to his owner. He dismisses any thought of reform and self-consciously brags that he will "take up wickedness--again, which was in my line," he says, "being brung up to it, and the other warn't . . . I might as well go the whole hog," he adds.[41] In abandoning himself to evil, Huck compounds the unspeakable sin of consigning himself to everlasting perdition.

But before he can "take up wickedness again" and rescue Jim, he seeks to warn the King and the Duke that the villagers are "on" to them. He is too late and finds the scoundrels being ridden out of town on the rail, tarred and feathered. They "didn't look like nothing in the world that was human . . . ."

> Well, it made me sick to see it; and I was sorry for them poor pitiful rascals, it seemed like I couldn"t ever feel any hardness against them anymore in the world. It was dreadful thing to see. Human beings <u>can</u> be awfully cruel to one another.⁴²

Huck's final view here is quite Calvinistic. Here is the depraved race--"Human beings <u>can</u> be awfully cruel to one another"--being treated with forgiveness or at least with pity, for the King and the Duke have been as malevolent and cruel in their dealings as are the people now maltreating them. It is also quite evident that total depravity need not, in Huck's words, be innate--human beings <u>can</u> be, not <u>are</u>. They can be perhaps if they are so trained by their social consciences, which reflects a rationalist's view of environment shaping the <u>tubula rasa</u>, something that Huck's very experience belies, for he has gone against the training of his environment--his good heart has won out over training because it is innately good. Nothing in this experience that we can see in the novel before his adventures with Jim tells us that Huck has been trained by his environment to regard the feelings or the well-being of others, much less those who have been hostile to him.

<u>Huckleberry Finn</u> projects a vision of life which focuses on the old Southwest, incorporating its glory and virtues, its decadence and depravity in "a varied series of frescoes of life along the . . . river and its 'sivilization.'"⁴³ Without

comment, Huck Finn paints a culture whose old values have gone to seed at least in part because those values had within them the seed of their own decay. River villagers are depicted as being "controlled by an outworn and debased Calvinism, and by a residue of the eighteenth century cult of sensibility."[44] These Bible-belters are, in general, characterized by folly, hypocrisy, bigotry, cruelty. Except, that is, for a few significant characters: Mary Jane Wilks, the Phelpses and notably the befuddled, kindly, well-intentioned Uncle Silas--not to mention the chief exceptions, Huck and Jim. Indeed this saving remnant belies the aging philosopher who harps on "the damned human race" or, more specifically, on man as "merely a machine automatically functioning."[45] Clemens can hardly write off mankind as all bad when he delineates a figure like Jim, a slave who exemplifies to perfection the loving father and friend, or like the warm-hearted, affectionate Huck, who morally and spiritually triumphs over his ghetto-like origins under the tutelage of his alcoholic, "nigger"-hating Pap and the "unco guid" Miss Watson. Compared to them, or to Grangerfords-Shepherdsons, the Brickvilleites, the Wilks's sisters' friends, etc., these two non-church goers shine forth as model Christians, "obedient to the golden rule and the commandment to love one's neighbor."[46]

Although the closing chapters of *Huck Finn*, the so-called "evasion" chapters with their burlesque of freeing Jim, indicate no new philosophical consideration on Clemens's part, they nevertheless point up his inability to adhere to a single philosophical stance. Certainly the closing chapters complete the frame with which the novel opens and are tonally compatible with the Tom Sawyer gang of cut-throats at the novel's beginning. And Huck himself does not undergo any radical transformation of character, though some critics are quick to point out his slowly nurtured sympathy for Jim seems to have been forgotten in the evasion chapters. Huck, as Michael Egan has clearly demonstrated, like Twain himself never entirely loses his racism.[47] Yet the evasion chapters are not in keeping with those depicting Huck's life after he leaves St. Petersburg, and countless reasons have been offered for the change. Clemens made clear that the beginning and the ending of the novel came easily for him, and both are tonally compatible. But Egan and others have seen the overt intent of the beginning of the novel to be heavily satirical, Egan specifically claiming that the novel was intended to illustrate the evils of slavery. It was begun in 1876, he says, "the year in which the victorious Northern Republicans reached their historic political compromise with the Southern Democrats, effectively reintroducing white supremacy in the old Confederacy. All the civil libertarian gains of the War were thus in practice wiped out, and racism and <u>de facto</u> slavery were back on the national agenda."[48] Though some of Egan's conclusions are open to question, he sees clearly enough that "the novel was also an act of graceful tribute to a way of life which, although considered by Twain to have been profoundly anachronistic, was nevertheless almost equally profoundly loved by him." Thus, Egan says, "It is a divided work of fiction, and this is why its moods alternate between bursts of nostalgia and cynicism."[49]

Twain seemed to write easily when he could write what was on his mind, and if Egan is correct that the political issues of 1876 prompted the early part of the novel, then it may well be that different political issues in 1883 when Clemens finished the novel account for the differences. Leo Marx sees the conclusion as a betrayal of the thrust of the novel in that Twain's scathing denunciation of a corrupt society depicted in the voyage down the river is repudiated by the closing chapters that implicitly exonerate that society.[50] Again, such inconsistency may very well be explained in several ways. Louis J. Budd aptly points out that "Always too demanding of human potentiality, Twain was increasingly nauseated by the machine politics that led to the Blaine-Cleveland election of 1884. But his European trip of 1878-1879 had refired his delight in the American freedom of movement and self-assertion that underlies Huckleberry Finn. His equations were complicated, unstable."[51]

Indeed they were. The satire of the American South that is the bulk of the novel, excluding the evasion chapters, is only partially offset by satire by Europe evident in Huck's commentary on European history and aristocracy. But Jay Martin points out that during the years between the start and the finish of Huck Finn, Twain experienced "temporary alienation from the New England worthies" and "disenchantment with travel abroad, especially with the French and English."[52] Perhaps then in 1882-1883 Clemens was experiencing again a nostalgia for that part of the South represented by the Quarleses so kindly depicted in the Phelp's Farm in the evasion chapters. Whatever the reasons, Millicent Bell is certainly correct in observing that "the book opposes all aspects of any dominant culture" and that Clemens suspected "that all social forms--not merely American Southern aristocratic ones--might be impositions," just as Huck Finn reveals Clemens's discomfort with any one philosophical form.[53]

What seems to finally happen at the conclusion of Huck Finn is comparable to what finally happens at the end of Connecticut Yankee; Twain undercuts himself. He spends the better part of a novel satirizing a society--in Huck it is the old South; in Yankee it is medieval society--and in the conclusion he allows the very society being satirized to conquer the satirist. In Yankee the conclusion is tragic; in Huck Finn the conclusion is comic; by neither are the critics made happy. Though the conclusion to Huck is artistically unacceptable, it certainly helps balance the harsh satire throughout the bulk of the novel. After all, Clemens did say around 1897 or 1898, ". . . in my experience hard-hearted people are very rare everywhere."[54]

Not only had Clemens examined and found wanting institutions, governments, and philosophies, he had no locus abroad or at home to which he could feel any more loyalty than to the seriously flawed South of his boyhood. He was a man without a home except for the home made for him by Livy, yet he was a man made welcome everywhere because he understood whatever he experienced, and he could, like the chameleon, fit those very intellectual and moral environments he found reasons to both accept and reject.

In many ways Huckleberry Finn does not present a consistent view of God, man, and the universe. But it should not. What is clear is that man's institutions have failed him. The church has created and fostered a false piety and an anti-rationalistic emotionalism that are destructive of humane goals. The government has created "unnatural" laws equally destructive. This does not argue for the abolition of religion and government; it does point out the difficulty of perceiving truth and leading a decent life dominated by such institutions. And certainly, man freed from these encumbrances of false religion and false government can come closer to truth, goodness, and God, as Huck and Jim come closer. But the god created by, prayed to, and feared in Calvinistic churches, the god paraded by missionaries before primitive people, and the government that condones and abets slavery and wheeler-dealer speculation in the gilded age are not the source of the "heart" that prevails over the "deformed conscience."

Nowhere else in Twain's work before or after is there the richness of texture to be found in Huckleberry Finn, a texture made possible by Twin's uncertainty about God, man, and the universe, an uncertainty beautifully balanced throughout. His later work is less successful not because he resolved the uncertainty but because he insisted on allowing his message to dominate art.

ENDNOTES TO CHAPTER VI

1. Bernard Devot, The Portable Mark Twain, p. 16.
2. Introduction to Adventures of Huckleberry Finn, p. xxii.
3. Smith, Introduction, p. xxiif.
4. What Is Man? and Other Essays (New York, Harper, 1924), p. 99.
5. Huckleberry Finn, p. 16.
6. Branch, Literary Apprenticeship of Mark Twain, p. 200.
7. Huckleberry Finn, p. 16.
8. Huckleberry Finn, p. 125.
9. Huckleberry Finn, p. 128.
10. Huckleberry Finn, p. 321; See Blair, Mark Twain & Huck Finn, p. 415, FN 11.
11. Blair, p. 416.
12. Blair, pp. 143-44.
13. Blair, pp. 143-44.
14. Blair, pp. 144.
15. Trilling, Huckleberry Finn, The Liberal Imagination (New York, Viking 1951), p. 111.
16. Huckleberry Finn, p. 152.
17. Huckleberry Finn, p. 169.
18. Autobiography, pp. 279-80.
19. Huckleberry Finn, p. 181.
20. Huckleberry Finn, p. 182.
21. Huckleberry Finn, p. 182.

22. *Huckleberry Finn*, p. 183.
23. *Huckleberry Finn*, p. 183.
24. *Huckleberry Finn*, pp. 193, 195.
25. *Huckleberry Finn*, p. 203.
26. *Huckleberry Finn*, p. 225.
27. *Huckleberry Finn*, p. 235.
28. *Huckleberry Finn*, p. 252.
29. *Huckleberry Finn*, p. 265.
30. *Huckleberry Finn*, p. 294.
31. *Huckleberry Finn*, p. 294.
32. *Huckleberry Finn*, pp. 294-95; see Carrington, *The Dramatic Unity of Huckleberry Finn*, (Columbus, Ohio State University Press, 1976), pp. 21, 26.
33. *Huckleberry Finn*, p. 295.
34. *Huckleberry Finn*, p. 295.
35. *Huckleberry Finn*, p. 295.
36. *Huckleberry Finn*, p. 296.
37. *Huckleberry Finn*, p. 296.
38. *Huckleberry Finn*, p. 296.
39. *Huckleberry Finn*, p. 297.
40. Blair, *Mark Twain & Huck Finn*, p. 143.
41. *Huckleberry Finn*, p. 297.
42. *Huckleberry Finn*, pp. 320-21.
43. William M. Gibson, *The Art of Mark Twain* (New York, Oxford University Press, 1976), p. 107.
44. Smith, *Mark Twain, The Development of the Writer*, p. 117.

45. Blair, <u>Mark Twain & Huck Finn</u>, p. 343.
46. Allison Ensor, <u>Mark Twain & The Bible</u> (Lexington, University of Kentucky Press, 1969), p. 96.
47. Michael Egan, <u>Mark Twain's "Huckleberry Finn": Race, Class and Society</u> (Sussex University Press, 1977), P. 80.
48. Egan, p. 67.
49. Egan, p. 67.
50. Leo Marx, "Mr. Eliot, Mr. Trilling, and <u>Huckleberry Finn</u>" <u>The American Scholar</u> 22 (1953), pp. 423-40.
51. Louise J. Budd, "'A Nobler Roman Aspect' of <u>Adventures of Huckleberry Finn,</u>" One Hundred Years of "<u>Huckleberry Finn,</u>" eds. Robert Sattlemeyer and J. Donald Crowley (Columbia, University of Missouri Press, 1985), p. 36.
52. Jay Martin, "The Genie in the Bottle: Huckleberry Finn in Mark Twain's Life, "<u>One Hundred Years of "Huckleberry Finn,</u>" p. 57.
53. Millicent Bell, "<u>Huckleberry Finn</u> and the Sleights of Imagination," <u>One Hundred Years of "Huckleberry Finn,"</u> p. 131.
54. Albert Bigelow Paine, ed., <u>Mark Twain's Autobiography</u>, Vol. I (New York and London, Harper & Brothers, 1929), p. 125.

CHAPTER VII: THE JEREMIADS

The fine balance Samuel Clemens had in making <u>Huckleberry Finn</u> was lost to him in the writing of the books that followed. From <u>Connecticut Yankee</u> and <u>Pudd'nhead Wilson</u>--focusing on human depravity and the force of environment--to <u>Joan of Arc</u>, a sentimental diatribe deifying a perfect mortal and castigating the rest of mankind, Twain worked into the years of his supposed despair. The later works fail, not because Twain resolved the problems of man, god, and the universe, but because he let those problems dominate his art or his preoccupation with these problems was greater than his creative energy. The lack of philosophical resolution that underlies <u>Huck Finn</u> becomes conscious in the later works; Twain becomes consciously moral, writing not as though he had a tale to tell but as though he had a sermon to preach.

Composed over nearly five years when he was engrossed in financing the Paige typesetter, <u>A Connecticut Yankee in King Arthur's Court</u> reveals Clemens's philosophical confusion more clearly than any previous work. DeVoto bluntly admitted that "The <u>Yankee</u> is a contradictory book."[1] Smith dwells upon "the inconsistencies in the thought and technique that mar a potential masterpiece."[2] Frederick found the tale "confused and confusing . . . notably inconsistent and self-contradictory."[3]

Obviously some of the contradiction in <u>Yankee</u> comes from

Twain's posing a problem for himself that he could not solve. Something had to destroy Hank Morgan's civilization so that at the end of the novel the reader can return to history. Arthur's court did not become the nineteenth century or the nineteenth century would not be the nineteenth century. Twain was forced to destroy the Boss's work to get a satisfactory conclusion to the fiction. The only question is who or what destroyed the 19th century in King Arthur's Court? Was it something in the Court or was it something in the nineteenth century? Or was it some mixing of the two for which the Boss alone would have to be responsible?

It is tempting too to regard the Boss as simply Mark Twain's mouthpiece, particularly because he often espouses Clemens's ideas, but it is important to remember that contradictions or inconsistencies in the Boss are not necessarily inconsistencies in the philosophy of the author. The Boss is a character, just as Huck is a character. That he is not as consistent a character as Huck is perhaps a consequence of his being a sophisticated man with all of the prejudices of the nineteenth century. His own century is a mess and he is attempting to make Arthur's world into his own nineteenth century mess, that is to substitute one mess for another. If the nineteenth century fails in Arthur's Court, perhaps it will not fail when its time comes.

This is not to say, of course, that the Boss's confusion does not reflect Clemens's own confusion; it probably does this and more, reflecting the confusion of the nineteenth century.

The Boss must fail and his failure should be accompanied by despair. And the despair at the end of <u>Yankee</u> may very well be Clemens's own. But that Clemens sees the failure of his own age and forces that failure on the Boss who arrogantly sees himself as a "giant among pygmies," does not necessarily mean that the twentieth or twenty-first centuries will fail or that mankind is doomed. Clemens was in the same hole he had been in and that scientific determinism had not helped him out of -- he did not know, he did not like what he saw, he hoped. And the Boss certainly reflects this confusion.

In 1883, two or three years before beginning work on <u>Yankee</u>, Clemens noted:

> I think we are only the microscopic trichina concealed in the blood of some vast creature's veins, and it is that vast creature whom God concerns himself about and not us.[4]

In 1886, another notebook entry elaborates:

> Special Providence! That phrase nauseates me-- with its implied importance of mankind and triviality of God. In my opinion these myriads of globes are merely the blood corpuscles flowing through the arteries of God and we but the animalculae that infest them, disease them, pollute them; and God does not know we are there and would not care if He did.[5]

Such deterministic thinking pervades <u>Yankee</u>, but it is contradicted by another thread of thought or attitude every bit as strong--the innate nobility of man. Often Clemens, consciously or otherwise, knotted these two strands as in considering a subject for a talk to the Hartford Monday Evening Club in 1889, the year that <u>Yankee</u> was published:

> Club Subject: The <u>insincerity</u> of man--all men are

liars, partial or hiders of facts, half tellers of
truths, shirks, moral sneaks. When a merely honest man
appears he is a comet--his fame is eternal--needs no
genius, no talent--mere honesty--Luther, Christ, etc.[6]

Clemens's opening Calvinistic generalization is denied in his second sentence. In short amid his heaviest involvement with finance, he still mulls over the problem of man and man's relation to God. <u>Yankee</u> is infused throughout with Clemens's confusion, much of which is most apparent in the character of Hank Morgan and in his efforts to remedy the evils in Arthur's Court--the church, the social system, the economic system and the government.

The arch villain is, of course, "that awful power, the Roman Catholic Church, [which] had converted a nation of men to a nation of worms."[7] The Boss's assumption here is that men are, if not innately noble, at least not negative ciphers that they must be "converted" to "worms," something less than they are in nature.

Not only is the Catholic Church an evil in itself, it is an evil that supports the other evils, notably the social system and government. The church "invented 'divine right of things,' and propped it all around . . . with the Beatitudes." To the common man, the church preached "humility, obedience to superior, the beauty of self-sacrifice; meekness under insult; patience, meanness of spirit, non-resistance under oppression" and the church "introduced heritable ranks and aristocracies, and taught all the Christian populations of the earth to bow down to them and worship them."[8] The Boss clearly sees how such systems have been allowed to continue when he notes

> Inherited ideas are a curious thing . . . I had mine, the king and his people had theirs. In both cases they flowed in ruts worn deep by time and habit, and the man who should have proposed to divert them by reason and argument would have had a long contract on his hands.[9]

The Boss does indeed propose to divert "inherited ideas" in his man-factories, institutions he has created for changing the thinking of the people, to prepare for the day when the revolution will be complete, the Church's power dispersed among Protestant churches, the social system made open-ended by joint stock companies, the government to change with the death of Arthur. But it does not occur to the Boss that what he would instill is as defective as what he is trying to replace, and indeed the final of the Boss's plans in not a failure of his ideas in themselves, but a failure to change the old order. It is the old order still; his veneer of nineteenth century civilization has been inadequate. This, perhaps, is the basic conflict in <u>Yankee</u>: the conflict between the all-powerful force of training and heredity against "reason and argument." Calvinistic scientific determinism versus romantic enlightenment.

It would be easy to see that the Boss moves from a position of confidence in his fellow man and his future to a position of despair, but such a movement is false. The Boss vacillates between these two positions throughout the fiction. The contradiction is made evident when the Boss assesses the causes of Morgan le Fay's brutality and viciousness: "Training--training is everything; training is all there is <u>to</u> a person."

To speak of nature "is folly" he says, "there is no such thing." What we call nature "is merely heredity and training. We have no thoughts of our own, no opinions of our own; they are transmitted to us, trained into us." Whatever "is original in us, and therefore fairly creditable or discreditable . . . , can be covered up and hidden by the point of a cambric needle, all the rest being atoms contributed by, and inherited from, a procession of ancestors" stretching back "to the Adam clan or grasshopper or monkey from whom our race has been so tediously and ostentatiously and unprofitably developed." As for himself, the Boss says, all he thinks about in "this plodding sad pilgrimage, this pathetic drift between the eternities, is to look out and humbly live a pure and high and blameless life, and save that one microscopic atom in me that is truly me: the rest may land in Sheol and welcome for all I care."[10] The Boss, showing every bit as much consistency as Twain, gives a capsule version of Clemens's theory of determinism to explain Morgan le Fay's viciousness. It is not her nature--there is no such thing--all she can lay credit or discredit to having original within her can be covered by the point of a cambric needle. She is the consequence of training. Here as elsewhere on the subject of determinism, Clemens generalizes that man is the plaything of forces beyond his control; but then he hedges. Training is everything, along with heredity--<u>except</u> the tiny speck which is original in us, that "one microscopic atom in me which is truly <u>me</u>" and which he wants to "save." Like Huck, the Boss has concluded that "there ain't no profit in it," but his very life contradicts his assertions. Can he really believe that "all he thinks about . . . is to look out and humbly live a pure and high and blameless life" and let the rest go to Sheol? Where is the humility in seeing himself a giant among pygmies? Does the Boss not see himself clearly? Does Twain see the Boss clearly? Is Twain aware of the self-contradiction? The pessimism inherent in the passage, the development of the race, "tedious," ostentatious," and "unprofitable," is denied in the Boss's decision to free Hugo, imprisoned by Morgan le Fay and tortured on the rack for having unlawfully killed the royal stag that was ravaging Hugo's crop. Hugo's wife has begged him to confess his guilt and be freed of his suffering by execution, sure to follow his confession. But Hugo refuses because by confessing he will have all his possessions confiscated and "leave wife and chick without bread and shelter . . . ." When the Boss learns this, he is overwhelmed by this selfless love and sacrifice and exclaims:

> Oh, heart of gold, now I see it! The bitter law takes the convicted man's estate and beggars his wife and orphans. They could torture you to death, but without conviction or confession they could not rob your wife and baby.[11]

This tribute to the "heart of gold" occurs three pages before the Boss explains why Morgan le Fay cannot be blamed; she was trained to believe as she does. Is the heart of gold also trained or is it just the microscopic speck, and if it is, isn't it enough? It is enough for the Boss who not only frees the sterling couple but books them for his colony--"in a Factory," he says "where I'm going to turn groping and grubbing automata into <u>men</u>."[12]

The Boss's obvious inconsistency in his pessimism is evidence that though Samuel Clemens could and did preach against the damned human race, he welcomed evidence that his belief in its damnation was unfounded. In fact, his daughter Clara cited evidence of such contradiction between his head and heart, how he preached one theory but acted on its contrary. In family discussions, she remarks, ". . . no subject interested my father more than the incorrigibility of the human race. Even unselfishness was selfish, because whatever the person did, he was doing to please himself." So long as the argument lasted, the human race was "irretrievably bad" to him. ". . . but in the next moment, if some caller recounted an incident picturing the noble conduct of a mother, husband, child, his eyes would fill with tears, and he would pace the floor, exclaiming: 'What noble generosity! that's a fine man for you!' Fortunately, his heart was fully as strong as his head. It could blaze with genuine emotion while his mind held to a logically formed idea."[13]

The Boss's inconsistency is evident in the very design of his revolution, a design that denies his own determinism. He talks with special pride of his plan to spread nineteenth century American Protestantism and freedom of religion. He has thought out each step of his brand new religious system, having already introduced, he says, " a complete variety of Protestant congregations," in which a person can be "any kind of Christian" he chooses. "I could have given my own sect the preference and made everybody a Presbyterian . . . but that would have been to affront a law of human nature: spiritual wants and instincts are as various in the human family as are physical appetites, complexions, and features," and men are only at their best, "morally, when . . . equipped with the religious garment whose color and shape and size" best fit "the spiritual complexion, angularities, and stature of the individual who wears it."[14] The Boss's concept of "man at his best, morally" certainly does not argue for a damned human race any more than the human family's "spiritual wants and instincts" argue for innate depravity.

What pains the Boss most is "the alacrity with which this oppressed community had turned their cruel hands against their own class in the interest of the common oppression" at the hands of an even crueler aristocracy. The charcoal burner, Marco, helped "to hang his neighbors, and had done his work with zeal, and yet was aware that there was nothing against them but a mere suspicion" and the Boss concludes that "this charcoal-burner was just the twin of the Southern 'poor white' of the far future." Such a comparison need not be seen as Twain's arguing for innate depravity, however, since the condition of the poor white, if not improved in Clemens's life after the Civil War, was not sufficient to allow for the continuance of slavery in the nineteenth century. In any event, Marco (and by implication the 'poor white') are not lost to humanity within the novel. And if Marco exemplifies what is wrong with man, his salvation must be seen as evidence of man's salvation. The Boss tests Marco bluntly by saying, "I think the devil's own work has been done last night upon those innocent people. The old baron got only what he deserved," and Marco blurts out,

> Even though you be a spy, and your words a trap for my undoing, yet are they such refreshment that to hear them . . . I would go to the gallows happy, as having had one good feast at least in a starved life. . . . I helped to hand my neighbors for that it was peril to my own life to show lack of zeal in the master's cause; the others helped for none other reason."[16]

This speech is evidence for the Boss that Marco is worth saving:

> There it was, you see. A man $\underline{is}$ a man, at bottom. Whole ages of abuse and oppression cannot crush the manhood clear out of him. . . . Yes, there is plenty good material for a republic in the most degraded people that ever existed--even the Russians . . .[17]

Such a conclusion is definitely at odds with the deterministic doctrine that <u>training</u> is everything, and Twain continues through the novel with a pattern of contradiction. He preaches determinism, then cites evidence against it or in favor of man's redeeming qualities. When later in the novel the slave-driver finally gives up trying to break the King's spirit, the Boss crows, "The fact is, the King was a good deal more than a king, he was a man . . ."[18] Quite obviously being a man is a noble condition a long way from depravity.

The Boss's man-factory reinforces his belief in the importance of "training." Thus the factories are to "turn out" men, but in selecting candidates for his factory the Boss chooses those who already show evidence of manhood--decency or independence of thought, people like Marco, people like Hugo, who are willing to die or to be tortured rather than continue with hypocrisy or hurt their loved ones.

Finally the Boss reveals his work "Slavery was dead and gone; all men were equal before the law; taxation had been equalized" and he awaits the death of his fried Arthur to establish a president, overthrow the Catholic Church and make his Republic complete.[19]

Then, when he is out of the country, the Boss is attacked by the Catholic Church and Arthur killed, and thus begins the holocaust. All his man factory products turn away from him, leaving him his "darling fifty-two" and Clarence as his sole allies against the age. He "touched the button," he says, "and shook the bones of England loose from her spine."[20] Instead of universal education, equality for all, religious freedom, there is mass murder and devastation, the common people resume their shackles, the Church is entrenched once more. In short, the age is left as it was found.

The holocaust at the end of Yankee may represent the nadir of pessimism in Twain's fiction at the time, ". . . the thing in man which makes him cruel to a slave is in him permanently and will not be rooted out in a million years."[21] Yet it is impossible to forget that there was a loyal fifty-two untainted by tradition. Are they different because they were trained from the cradle or because they were born with that "microscopic atom" that made them different from the rest?

In his The Veracious Imagination, Cushing Strout observes that "any close reader must be puzzled by the Yankee's final expression of a yearning nostalgia for the very order he has been ridiculing and subverting throughout the story." Strout notes that Justin Kaplan in bringing "to the surface the rich tangle of emotional ties between 'The Private History of a Campaign that Failed'" and Connecticut Yankee calls "our attention to the implicit parallels [sic] in the novel between Arthur's England and the American South, between the Yankee's republican, industrial 'new deal' program and the ideology of the victorious North, between the two civil wars which, both in history and in the fiction, destroy an old order." Kaplan's correlations, Strout says, "tell us . . . about the raging ambivalence in the novelist's Southern and Northern loyalties, a conflict that turned his novel into a 'curse on both parts of the "contrast" and ended his battle of ancients and moderns with a double defeat.'"[22]

Kaplan's crucial connection between "The Private History of the Campaign that Failed" and Yankee is Twain's remark in a reading of the memoir in 1887 that the killing of an innocent civilian was the only battle in the history of the world where the opposing force was "utterly exterminated," which Kaplan points out describes precisely the conclusion of Yankee. Strout adds that both pieces "end exactly the same way with a Yankee in the arms of Mark Twain and each dying man is mumbling about his wife and children."[23]

It is difficult to disagree with Kaplan's conclusions of Yankee becoming a defeat of both cultures and for the reasons he suggests. By 1887, Clemens had seen enough of the world to find no institution he could accept without serious qualification. All of the mixed good and evil he found in the world and within himself. Nothing was pure. He had grown up in the South and he saw its evil in slavery and its virtue in idealism. He had found the North with its condemnation of slavery and its hypocrisy and crass materialism that engendered the Gilded Age. His regional loyalties were not with North, South, East, or West. He had been to Europe and found a high culture and an unacceptable aristocracy. As he later wrote in a letter a few months after his wife's death in 1904 describing himself as "a man without a country," "Wherever Livy was, that was my country. And now she is gone."[24] Mark Twain had become the chameleon, fitting in everywhere but belonging nowhere except to his family.

The ambivalence resulting in what Kaplan correctly calls the "curse" on both ancient and modern civilization in Yankee may well be a consequence not just of Twain's rejection of ancient and modern but an acceptance and an inclusion of both, which can explain Strout's "yearning nostalgia." Macnaughton suggests a reason for the ambivalence in Yankee by explaining the causes of the difficulties in reading Twain's late work Christian Science, specifically the "barriers" imposed in "the tonal variations in the greatment" of Mary Baker Eddy, variations from "supercilious contempt" to "awestruck wonder and fear." Macnaughton explains that "These variations can be explained both in terms of Mark Twain's perception of the woman's complexity and the manner in which she was regarded: she was worshipped by her followers, hence the writer's attempts to make her seem puny and ludicrous; non-Christian Scientists had a lack of respect for, and were ignorant of, her potentialities, hence Mark Twain's almost hyperbolic appreciation of her past and present achievements and his stress on her future capabilities."[25] This Macnaughton sees as merely another example of Mark Twain the radical "being undercut by Mark Twain the conservative." Episodes such as those found in "The Chronicle of Young Satan" "help explain why he was unable to commit himself totally to the kind of satiric stance that his critics would have had him assume. He recognized that there was often value in the man and institutions that he might have wished to tear down. Moreover, he recognized the impossibility of predicting all the results of even the most well-meaning social action."[26] What Clemens knew when he wrote Christian Science and "The Chronicle of Young Satan" he knew by the time he wrote Huckleberry Finn and Connecticut Yankee.

From a recognition of Clemens's inability to not see value in that which he wished to tear down and an inability to predict "all the results of even the most well-meaning social action" we can move to further illuminating parallels between The Mysterious Stranger and Connecticut Yankee. It might be said that Yankee is a working out in history of what Twain would later attempt to work philosophically in The Mysterious Stranger. Hank Morgan is the "giant among pygmies," the god of Yankee, as Satan is the god of Stranger. Satan's description of man's ending, that he "departs as stench," coincides perfectly with the conclusion of *Yankee* and the "poisonous air bred by those dead thousands."[27] The "utter annihilation" wreaked by Morgan is identical to those undergone by the little communities that Satan creates in the second and third chapters of *Stranger*. In Chapter II, Satan "reached out and took the heavy board seat out of our swing and brought it down and mashed all those people into the earth just as if they had been flies."[28] Again in Chapter II, after bringing a storm upon another such community, "in the midst of the howling of the wind and volleying of the thunder the magazine blew up, the earthquake rent the ground wide, and the castle's wreck and ruin tumbled into the chasm, which swallowed it from sight, and closed upon it, with all that innocent life, not one of the five hundred poor creatures escaping."[29] Satan is god in *Stranger* and as god he is creator. If he destroys these communities, he has created them. What is suggested here is the power of the artist over his work; as the narrator of *Stranger* tells us of Satan, "he made things live before you when he told about them," which of course is what the artist must achieve.[30] And like the artist novelist, Satan has the power of life and death in creating the lives that populate his story. Like the artist but unlike the mortal Hank Morgan, Satan knows "what the consequences are going to be--always."[31] Satan tells the narrator, "'I have wrought well for the villagers, though it does not look like it on the surface. Your race never knows good fortune from ill. You are always mistaking the one for the other. It is because they cannot see into the future."[32] Hank Morgan cannot foresee the results of his "new deal," and mistakes his interference for good. But what Satan clearly sees from his cosmic stance--"'What I am doing for the villagers will bear good fruit some day; in some cases to themselves; in other, to unborn generations of men.'"--the young narrator does not; "He didn't seem to know any way to do a person a favor except by killing him or making a lunatic out of him."[33] It is this cosmic perspective that allows Satan to urge laughter at the history of the world, the same unbound by time laughter that Merlin is frozen in after predicting Hank Morgan's thirteen centuries of sleep that will return him to the nineteenth century and wondering Which Was the Dream.

It is impossible to find a consistent attitude in the novel. It ends pessimistically in part because it must, but it cannot be said to be a final expression of despair; there are too many good people in it.

In Pudd'nhead Wilson (written in Italy in 1892-1894, and published in 1894) Twain pursues more decisively the theme of determinism so apparent in Connecticut Yankee. Once more the setting is a town located not a hundred miles above St. Louis; like Hannibal and St. Petersburg, Dawson's Landing is described as a town "washed by the clear waters of the great river,"[34] a collection of modest one and two story frame dwellings whose white-washed fronts are almost concealed by rosevines, honeysuckles, and morning glories. But the prettiness is spurious, for this description of Dawson's Landing introduces a tale of slavery, stark and foreboding, in a society presided over by a New World aristocracy no better than the old world one of Connecticut Yankee.

This aristocracy is led by Virginia-born York Leicester Driscoll whose religion is to be "a gentleman without stain or blemish," and whose religion must yield if he finds it in conflict with "the highest duty of his life."[35] He and his younger brother Percy Northumberland Driscoll, his best friend Pembroke Howard, and Colonel Cecil Burleigh Essex are the principal slave owners, each in his own way responsible for the "misery, suffering and hatred" of the tragedy in Pudd'nhead Wilson.[36] The comic pretentiousness of the aristocratic names openly ridicules the old southern slave-owning gentry, that same class being idealized by Howells in A Hazard of New Fortunes and by Henry Adams in Democracy. These writers, like Twain disgusted by a corrupt society exemplified by the Grant administration, may well have been looking backward longingly for a source of higher values. Twain in looking back saw no higher values in an old aristocratic South. Indeed the novel focuses upon Southern slavery's two ugliest sides, miscegenation and "being sold down the river." In answering once more the question "what is man?" Twain's answer is even grimmer than in Connecticut Yankee.

The novel virtually condemns the whole society of Dawson's Landing. Pudd'nhead Wilson, the novel's only aristocrat in the Jeffersonian sense--not of "the best blood of the Old Dominion"[37] but a man enlightened by marked character and ability--is ruined on his first day in town when the townsmen in their stupidity misunderstand his off-beat humor and put him down as a "pudd'nhead." Other vagaries of Wilson's character, his belonging to the Free-Thinkers' Society, verify further the town's first hasty conclusion.

Counterpoised against Wilson is Roxanna, Percy Driscolls's uneducated twenty-year old slave girl, "white as anybody, but the sixteenth of her which was black outvoted the other fifteen parts and made her a negro."[38] Roxy is an interesting amalgam of natural and acquired characteristic. She is "naturally" endowed with

> majestic form and structure . . . gestures and movements distinguished by a noble and stately grace . . . her complexion was very fair, with the rosy glow of vigorous health in her cheeks, her face was full of character and expression, her eyes were brown and liquid, . . . Her face was shapely, intelligent, and comely--even beautiful.[39]

And unlike Dawson's white yokelry, Roxy has the native intelligence to spot Wilson's power of mind: "'Dey calls him a pudd'nhead, en says he's a fool . . . He's de smartest man in dis town. . . .'"[40]

But if nature has been generous to Roxy, society has been less so. Her everyday garb is "dis mis'able ole linsey woolsey" and her new Sunday gown "a cheap curtain-calico, a conflagration of gaudy colors and fantastic figures."[41] Though she has "an easy, independent carriage," as well as a high and "sassy" way among her own caste, she is "meek and humble enough where white people were."[42] Finally, her speech bears the indelible mark of her bondage.

And though Roxy represents powerful emotional values in her love for her son and her monumental sacrifices to keep him from being sold down the river, they are values which have, as Smith says, "survived the perverted training" of slavery in Dawson's Landing. She is not so fortunate in escaping her masters' pride of ancestry, their code of honor, even their contempt of Negroes," as Smith again points out.[43]

On the day that "Pudd'nhead" Wilson first comes to town, two baby boys are born in the home of Percy Driscoll, the Driscolls's son Thomas A. Beckett Driscoll and Roxy's newborn Valet de Chambre, later called "Chambers." When Mrs. Driscoll dies and Percy Driscoll threatens to sell his house slaves down the river, Roxy protects her son by switching him with the Driscoll child and Twain has thus laid the foundation for his plot that will prove "training is everything." Roxy, like Huck Finn in a critical moment, "knowed she done wrong," but unlike Huck she squares with her conscience without a hitch: "'Tain't no sin-- white folks has done it!'" And she adds, even the Lord saves and condemns: "'He do jis' as he's a mineter,'" bestowing free grace on saint or sinner. She knows this form"'. . . dat old nigger preacher dat tole it, de time he came over here fum Illinois en preaced in de nigger church.'"[44] Roxy's precedents for her act--white folks and their Calvinist deity--demonstrate a debased culture corrupting both master and slave.

The training both children receive is disastrous to their lives. The real Tom Driscoll, living as a black and a slave and called "Chambers," adopts the slave's attitudes, especially toward his young master; he learns to be "meek and docile," no matter how "fractious" or overbearing "Tom" is to him.[45] For Tom "Cuffed and banged and scratched Chambers unrebuked . . ." Mr. Percy Driscoll himself "told Chambers that under no provocation whatever was he privileged to lift his hand against his little master."[46] Such upbringing indoctrinates the real Tom Driscoll with the ideology of slavery so successfully that at the end when he resumes his rightful role as an aristocrat he can't "unlearn the slave idiom" or feel at home in his new social position.

In consequence of his training as a white aristocrat, "Tom" is spoiled rotten, drinks, gambles, stays in debt, lords it over others, and deceives everybody. As a youth when "Chambers" saves him from drowning in the river, Tom reciprocates by trying first to cut Chambers' throat and then to persuade his father to sell him down the river. And he has just as maliciously taught Roxy "her place." Roxy soon learns better than to venture a motherly "caress or fondling epithet in his quarter," no matter how much she feels the need for it. To him, such affection "from a nigger" is so repulsive that he warns her "to keep her distance and remember who she was."[47] His viciousness is climaxed by selling his heroic mother down the river and by the murder of his adoring foster-uncle for his money.

The training the two boys receive illustrates the point that

Twain would make: "Training is everything." But the result of training in <u>Pudd'nhead</u> is more ominous than that the Boss attempted in <u>Yankee</u>. The Boss's failure to produce "men" from his factories came from his inability to erase the influence of the Church; nevertheless, the victims of the Church's powerful influence were at least threatened by the Boss's plan for reform. But in <u>Pudd'nhead</u> Twain removes the threat to the institution, and spiritlessness is never challenged. The training has taken, and the "man" has been lost.

An early outline of the novel pictures the false Tom Driscoll to be morally monstrous because he has grown up a slave. Anne P. Wigger points out that Twain's original purpose was partly to demonstrate "the influence of inherited training . . . Tom is base because of the effect of slave-owning . . . brutal because of slave-owning heredity . . . Cowardly because the Negro blood in him has had to submit to generations of subjugation. Slavery itself, acting on generations of slaves and slave-owners is the corrupting force in Tom's nature." Although in the final draft this role is played down and the material treating the hereditary influence of slavery is largely omitted, Wigger correctly concludes,

> . . . it is important to recognize Tom as an intended representative of the moral decay which arises from slavery, for to consider him base simply because of his Negro blood is to ignore the central purpose of this book--an ironical examination of slavery.[48]

Certainly the irony in the novel is great and the condemnation of slavery is thorough, but Twain has also tried to support his point about training, and in making the cynical maxims of Pudd'nhead Wilson a chorus-like commentary on the times, he provides his grimmest indictment so far of the creature man.

The bleakness of Pudd'nhead Wilson should anticipate even darker writing in Clemens's next work, for life had become no easier for him in the interval. But after the failure of his publishing company, he was ready to shout, as he wrote his wife in January 1894,

> "Farewell-a long farewell--to business! I will never touch it again!"
> "I will live in literature, I will wallow in it, revel it, I will swim in ink! Joan of Arc--but this is premature; the anchor is not down yet."[49]

And that Twain wrote Joan to avoid a grim world seems fairly evident from a letter to Mrs. Fairbanks in January, 1893 when he says it

> . . . is private & not for print, it's written for love and not for lucre, & to entertain the family with, around the lamp by the fire (the day's chapter of the tale, the day's product of "work" as this sort of literary dreaming has been miscalled) . . .[50]

In short, Sam Clemens put his heart and soul into Joan of Arc and may well have left his intelligence out, because he felt a compulsive need to escape from not only the plague of business at which he had failed wretchedly but also the darkness of the world outside his family. His very intentional splitting of these two worlds--the family, the private and the other, the public-- reflects Twain's division of self for public and private uses; his intellect, wit, and satire for public--his heart, warmth, and love for his family. Both are real. The result is predictable.

A novel of blatant melodrama, with everything reduced to a conflict between Hero and Villain--angelic heroism versus satanic villainy. Thus Joan of Arc and her adversaries are falsified into stereotypes and not one of the <u>dramatis personae</u> emerges as a fleshed out character.

The authorial idolatry is announced in the translator's preface: "She was perhaps the only entirely unselfish person whose name has a place in profane history."[51] Whatever else it may be, such praise is strange coming from a disillusioned writer whose philosophy presupposes mankind's innate selfishness. The narrator may avow "I am not going to distort or discolor the facts of this miserable trial,"[52] but in using the word "miserable" he belies his intent. Mark Twain, moralist-sentimentalist, must side with Indestructible Innocence against Implacable Evil, whatever his promise to the contrary.

The villain is the highest French society "foul in both" mind and body, lords and princes who made that "infamous era . . . stand aghast at the spectacle of their atrocious lies black with unimaginable treacheries, butcheries, and bestialities."[53] The villain is the Church represented by the Bishop, "that bastard of Satan, Pierre Cauchon."[54]

To Roger Salomon, <u>A Connecticut Yankee</u> points the way to what he calls its creator's ultimate negation and <u>Yankee</u> led directly to <u>Joan of Arc</u>, in which Clemens is "driven to escape imaginatively from the nightmarish implications of his own rational formulations." Thus <u>Joan</u> represents Clemens's "final desperate attempt to establish values apart from the futile treadmill of sin and suffering which constituted man's life on earth." But Salomon goes on to say that there is "but one short step from <u>Joan of Arc</u> to <u>The Mysterious Stranger</u>--from a belief in the goodness, however meaningless ultimately, of one isolated individual to a belief in the corruptibility of all humanity."[55]

Whatever Salomon sees Clemens's ultimate belief to be, he implicitly finds "a belief in the goodness," in keeping with the conclusion that in <u>Joan of Arc</u> Clemens's "long search for perfection in mankind is culminated. Faith in the human species was possible."[56] Robert Wiggins echoes such an assessment of <u>Joan's</u> value to Clemens in noting that in the novel Twain found evidence of "the perfectibility of mankind . . . the sole concrete argument against the pessimistic doctrines of his deterministic philosophy."[57]

Such conclusions seem partial and premature. Certainly in the character of Joan, Twain has countered any Calvinistic claim to innate depravity, a depravity that extends to almost everyone else but Joan, and he has allowed himself a vacation from the mental strain of providing the motive of "training" that had to account for evil in a Morgan le Fay or the false Tom Driscoll. What must not be forgotten is the uniqueness of Joan in Twain's work--"it is private and not for print . . . this sort of literary dreaming." If it is dreaming, it is conclusive evidence that Clemens has not yet found permanent despair. On the other hand, the vicious portrayal of a rotten social fabric makes equally clear that though Twain may have produced a "literary dream" it is soiled with the world's evil.

Samuel Clemens has now passed through and partially incorporated doctrines of Calvinism, romanticism, the Enlightenment, and the scientific determinism of his own age. He remains intellectually pessimistic and emotionally committed to the human race. He continues to oscillate between mind and heart, pessimism and hope in the period that is supposed to mark his final despair.

ENDNOTES TO CHAPTER VII

1. DeVoto, "Mark Twain and the Limits of Criticism," Forays and Rebuttals (Freeport, New York: Books for Libraries Press, 1970, 1936), pp. 373-403.
2. Smith, Mark Twain: the Development of a Writer, p. 138; Mark Twain's Fables of Progress, p. 5.
3. Frederick, The Darkened Sky, p. 156.
4. Twain, Notebooks, p. 170.
5. Twain, Notebooks, p. 190.
6. Twain, Notebooks, p. 181.
7. Twain, A Connecticut Yankee in King Arthur's Court, IX (Author's Edition), pp. 64-65.
8. Connecticut Yankee, p. 65.
9. Connecticut Yankee, p. 63.
10. Connecticut Yankee, p. 150.
11. Connecticut Yankee, p. 147.
12. Connecticut Yankee, p. 147.
13. Clara Clemens, My Father, Mark Twain (New York, Harper & brothers, 1931), p. 183.
14. Connecticut Yankee, p. 77.
15. Connecticut Yankee, pp. 298-99.
16. Connecticut Yankee, p. 301.
17. Connecticut Yankee, p. 301.
18. Connecticut Yankee, p. 355.
19. Connecticut Yankee, pp. 398-400.

20. <u>Connecticut Yankee</u>, p. 433.
21. <u>Notebooks</u>, p. 198; see Baetzhold, <u>Mark Twain and John Bull</u>, p. 160.
22. Cushing Strout, <u>The Veracious Imagination</u> (Middletown, Wesleyan University Press, 1981), p. 283.
23. Cushing Strout, p. 282.
24. John S. Tuckey, <u>Mark Twain's Which Was the Dream</u> (Berkeley and Los Angeles, University of California Press, 1967), p. 23.
25. William R. Macnaughton, <u>Mark Twain's Last Years as a Writer</u> (Columbia & London, University of Missouri Press, 1979), p. 192.
26. Macnaughton, p. 139.
27. Mark Twain, <u>The Mysterious Stranger</u> (New York and London, Harper & Brothers, 1929), p. 26.
28. <u>The Mysterious Stranger</u>, p. 17.
29. <u>The Mysterious Stranger</u>, p. 21.
30. <u>The Mysterious Stranger</u>, p. 19.
31. <u>The Mysterious Stranger</u>, p. 77.
32. <u>The Mysterious Stranger</u>, p. 81.
33. <u>The Mysterious Stranger</u>, p. 81, 131.
34. Twain, <u>Pudd'nhead Wilson</u>, p. 2.
35. <u>Pudd'nhead</u>, p. 102.
36. Geismar, p. 136.
37. <u>Pudd'nhead</u>, p. 103.
38. <u>Pudd'nhead</u>, p. 12.

39. *Pudd'nhead*, pp. 11-12.
40. *Pudd'nhead*, pp. 23-24.
41. *Pudd'nhead*, p. 19.
42. *Pudd'nhead*, p. 12.
43. *Pudd'nhead*, p. 177.
44. *Pudd'nhead*, p. 22.
45. *Pudd'nhead*, p. 28.
46. *Pudd'nhead*, p. 29.
47. *Pudd'nhead*, p. 33.
48. Anne P. Wigger, "The Composition of Mark Twain's *Pudd'nhead Wilson and Those Extraordinary Twins*: Chronology and Development," *Modern Philology*, Vol. LV (November 1957), p. 96.
49. Twain, *Letters*, II, 607.
50. *Mark Twain to Mrs. Fairbanks*, ed. Dixon Wecter (San Marino, California: Huntington Library, 1949), p. 269.
51. *Joan of Arc*, p. xif.
52. *Joan of Arc*, p. 120.
53. *Joan of Arc*, xif.
54. *Joan of Arc*, p. 110.
55. Roger Salomon, *Twain and the Image of History*, p. 189.
56. Mentor L. Williams, "Mark Twain's 'Joan of Arc,'" *Michigan Alumnus Quarterly*, Vol. 54 (May 8, 1948), p. 245.
57. Robert A. Wiggins, *Mark Twain: Jackleg Novelist* (Seattle: University of Washington, 1964), pp. 112-13.

CHAPTER VIII: THE MYTH OF MARK TWAIN'S FINAL DESPAIR

In 1895, Samuel Clemens reflected:

> It is the strangest thing that the world is not full of books that scoff at the pitiful world, and the useless universe and violent, contemptible human race--books that laugh at the whole paltry scheme and deride it. Curious, for millions of men die every year with these feelings in their hearts. Why don't I write such a book? Because I have a family. There is no other reason. Was this those other people's reasons?[1]

Van Wyck Brooks took Sam Clemens literally and drew the simple conclusion that he was a moral coward not to tell his own public the bitter pessimistic truth of his encounter with the world. Certainly Clemens had the causes for despair that DeVoto enumerated:

> His publishing firm failed; his fortune and his wife's were dissipated in the failure of the Paige typesetting machine; his health broke and, a bankrupt at the age of sixty, he had to make a heartbreaking effort to pay off his debts; his oldest daughter died; his youngest daughter developed epilepsy; his wife declined into permanent invalidism.[2]

As a consequence, DeVoto says, "His world toppled in ruins round him, all the bases of his belief were called into question, and his talent was so impaired that for a long time it seemed to have been destroyed. When at last it was integrated again . . . There is a new Mark Twain, the author of What Is Man? and The Mysterious Stranger."[3] These two works and the Autobiography, DeVoto says,

> are essentially the same thing. They are an interpretation of personal tragedy, a confession of guilt, a plea for understanding and pardon, a defiance

> of fate, and a judgment passed on mankind and its place in the universe. . . . they represent not a complete change certainly, for their elements were always in him though held in the healthy equilibrium of his artistic success and personal happiness, but a new orientation of his personality and a new if minor expression of his genius.[4]

DeVoto's conclusions are echoed in Hamlin Hill's assessment that

> Until 1900 Mark Twain managed to retain control over his universe, over his despair, pessimism, frustration, and insensitivity, by his artistic capacity. . . . Something occurred which made the adversity and the conflicts no longer convertible into finished art. Age . . . The death of his most sensitive critic . . . And the junkyard of unfinished manuscripts and ill-conceived literary ideas was the most enduring testimony of the failure of Mark Twain to retain creative control over his world.[5]

The final result, Hill says, is that "The bitterness which permeated What Is Man? "Letters from the Earth," the "Mysterious Stranger" fragments, much of the autobiography, and most of the shorter political writings was a rage at the obscenity of life."[6] Though it is far from his intent, even John S. Tuckey contributes to the notion of final bitter despair in the last years of Twain's life in his Mark Twain's Which Was the Dream? Compiling mostly previously unpublished work written between 1896 and 1905, Tuckey notes that "Their principle fable is that of a man who has been long favored by luck while pursuing a dream of success that has seemed about to turn into reality. Sudden reverses occur and he experiences a nightmarish time of failure. He clutches at what may be a saving thought: perhaps he is indeed living in a nightmare from which he will awaken to his former felicity. But there is also the possibility that what seems a dream of disaster may be the actuality of his life."[7] Tuckey makes clear that much of the material collected in his book "was written with pleasure," but the "dream" motive of failure that Twain seemed consumed by for several years around 1900 was finally unproductive and supports the contention of artistic failure.[8]

Admittedly the elder Clemens often engaged in bitter pessimism, even nihilistic-sounding reflection; evidence that he did just that is overwhelming. But such pessimism and reflection are evident in <u>Joan of Arc</u>, <u>Connecticut Yankee</u>, <u>Huckleberry Finn</u>, and even in <u>Innocents Abroad</u>. They are not limited to the works of the aging Clemens and more importantly they are not and never were the whole of his bent, do not add up to "absolute negation . . . nihilism,"[9] as those critics echoing Brooks or DeVoto have insisted. Such criticism does not recognize the eclecticism of Sam Clemens's religious outlook, the deep-rooted contradictions originating early in life and never resolved, which lie behind his life-long rebellion against a Calvinistic God, the stern orthodox, watered-down Calvinism in his Southwestern frontier community and its cardinal belief in human depravity, the equally heterodox religion of the Enlightenment he got from his father's Deism and his favorite Uncle John Quarles'more radical deistic faith, Universalism.

The fact is, as Budd says, Samuel Clemens never actually retreated into "total darkness and despair."[10] If he used Satan as a device in <u>The Mysterious Stranger</u> to harp on such favorite targets as "the paltry and debased nature of man and the indifference and malignity of the deity," as Fussell points out

[11] such emotional reactions did not convey his whole response to life; they merely rid him of his pent-up venom against the tyrannical, Big Brother God of Calvinism absorbed as a boy in Hannibal and generally accepted by the damned human race. These latter-day "eruptions" alternated with moments in which his intuitive sense of the reality of virtue and man's potential self-betterment shone through. This pursuit of virtue, this search for faith in the inherent goodness of mankind, undergirds his latter-day fulminations, his humor-as-satire, which he used to goad fallen man on to reform. Twain never ceased to use this weapon against man's folly and evil. As Tuckey says, ". . . this notion of a sustained despair is beginning to look like a disposable myth of Mark Twain's criticism,"[12] and the weakness of the myth is evident in the affirmation inherent in the late writings of Mark Twain, the documents of despair themselves.

<u>What Is Man</u>?, Mark Twain's self-styled Bible of determinism, is not a despairing document, though many have found it to be such. The book opens with an Old Man and a Young Man engaged in a dialogue on the nature of man. Tiresomely the old man repeats that man is a machine:

> Whatsoever a man is, is due to this make, and to the <u>influences</u> brought to bear upon it by his heredities, his habitat, his associations. He is moved, directed, COMMANDED, by <u>exterior</u> influences--solely. He originates nothing himself--not even an opinion, not even a thought.[13]

The Young Man rejects the assertion as nonsense, asking in substance, where did I form my opinion that you are talking foolishness? To which the Old Man has a ready answer, ". . . <u>you</u>

did not form that one; your machinery did it for you-automatically . . ." Not even Shakespeare created his plays. "<u>He was a machine</u>, and machines do not create." True, he was Gobeline loom, whereas "you and I are but sewing machines."[14] "It is an infamous doctrine," the Young Man indignantly replies. "It isn't a doctrine, it is merely a fact," the old man says, and then seems to contradict himself by asserting that the Young Man or the human race can change its ways for the better. The Young Man remarks that the cowardly man may undertake to conquer his cowardice and may even succeed, so, he asks, what does that show? Here the Old Man drops the analogy of man-the machine and answers, ". . . it shows the value of <u>training in the right directions</u> . . ."

> Inestimably valuable is training, influence, education, in the right directions--<u>training one's self-approbation</u> to elevate its ideals.[15]

He reminds the neophyte in emphatic language:

> <u>From the cradle to his grave a man never does a single thing which has any</u> FIRST AND FOREMOST <u>object but one--to secure peace of mind, spiritual comfort, for</u> HIMSELF.[16]

Even the noble passion of patriotism, love of country, is based on the law of "<u>the approval of his neighbors and the public</u>."[17] Not only that, the Old Man observes, a mother's love for her child simply shows that the mother follows the law of her make, that motherly self-sacrifice does not exist.[18]

Then the Old Man shifts his terms and drops the machine-man metaphor to emphasize the training of the Conscience, "that independent Sovereign, that insolent absolute Monarch inside of a man who is the man's Master." It is that mysterious autocrat, lodged in a man, which compels the man to content its desires. It may be called the Master Passion--the hunger for Self-Approval."[19] Men and women, he says, good or bad, spend their lives contenting it. True, Conscience represents the training of "parents, teachers, the pulpits, and books . . . a million unnoticed influences," and, he admits, "A conscience can be trained to shun evil and prefer good."[20] Yet he later says we are all slaves to this Interior Monarch which embodies the ideas and ideals trained into us, but which can be changed for the better: "<u>Training</u> is potent. Training toward higher, and higher, and ever higher ideals is worth any man's thought and labor and diligence."[21] Surely an indication of how far at variance the Old Man is now from the sense of his original metaphor is in his "Admonition": "From the cradle to the grave, during all his waking hours, the human being is under training, . . . Man is a chameleon; by the law of his nature he takes the color of his place of resort. The influences about him create his preferences, his aversions, his politics, his tastes, his morals, his religion."[22] This very chameleonness is his "greatest good fortune. He has only to change his habitat--his <u>associations</u> [though] the impulse to do it must come from the outside--he cannot originate it himself, with purpose in view. Sometimes a very small thing, however, can furnish him the initiatory impulse and start him on a new road, with a new ideal." For example, "the chance reading of a book can make him shift to new associations in sympathy with his new ideals" and result in "an entire change of his way of life"[23]

A secret of such life-changes is laying "traps for people. Traps baited with <u>Initiatory Impulses toward high ideals</u>," just what "a missionary does," or "what government ought to do," because "To train men to lead virtuous lives is an inestimably important thing."[24] Thus the essence of the Old Man's "gospel," far from being negative, deterministic, or finally nihilistic, is set forth in his "plan for the general betterment of the race's condition," as training

> . . . your ideals <u>upward</u> and <u>still upward</u> toward a summit where you will find your chiefest pleasure in conduct which, while contenting you, will be sure to confer benefits upon your neighbor and the community.[25]

This is not a "new gospel," the Old Man insists, but one that has been taught "ten thousand years by [all] the great religions--all the great gospels"; its only claim to newness, its honesty without concealment, its recognition of "the supreme and absolute Monarch that resides in man" that must be "conciliated and contented first [for] right living."[26] At this point, the author appears to realize suddenly that he is writing a moral tract on "a self-training machine" rather than piecing together his deterministic gospel; hence his alter ego, the Old Man, shifts back to the man-machine figure, as Jones has pointed out.[27]

Twain's biographer pointed up the original problem:

> Once admitting the postulate, that existence is merely a sequence of cause and effect beginning with the primal atom, and we have a theory that must stand or

fall as a whole. We cannot say that man is a creature of circumstance, even in the minutest fractional degree.[28]

And later commentators on <u>What Is Man</u>? have noted this same inconsistency. Over a half century ago, the British psychologist and friend of the aged Clemens, Sir John Adams, remonstrated that after the determinist has reduced us to a machine, he starts preaching to us. ". . . nobody could find the least fault with it had it come from a pulpit or an ordinary 'improving' book. But what has it to do here? . . . it is impossible to apply Mark's admonition, if we accept his general theory as laid down in his book . . ."[29] In his doctoral dissertation, Frank C. Flowers went farther, attempting to show that Twain believed in moral freedom because he devotes about two-thirds of <u>What Is Man</u>? to "training the machine" rather than emphasizing pessimism and despair.[30]

"The standard modern analysis" of <u>What Is Man</u>?, as Baender calls Jones's article, expresses agreement. "This concept of a self-training machine may be untenable as a philosophical doctrine," Jones remarks.[31] Jones also questions DeVoto's thesis that <u>What Is Man</u>? is "a product of Twain's final pessimism and despair," but does agree that Mark Twain wrote his "gospel" in a desperate effort to secure peace of mind after pondering it for a quarter of a century. Determinism might prove a refuge for the ravages of his "trained Presbyterian conscience."[32]

But the work itself, <u>What Is Man</u>?, is almost a Rorschach test of those who read it. Twain's old friend Andrew Carnegie, not knowing who wrote the book, sensed its affirmation: "I don't see that it goes much deeper than we were before. . . . 'All is well since all grows better.' Our only duty is to obey the Judge within."[33] But a New York *Times* reviewer noted that there "is nothing new in pessimism of this kind."[34] And still another alluded to the book's "pitch-black pessimism," and insisted that Clemens's "lack of training and skill as a philosopher is nothing against Mark Twain," because we value him for his humor and satire.[35] Finally Waldo Frank dismissed *What Is Man?* in 1919 as "the profane utterance of a defeated soul,"[36] and the myth of Twain's final despair was half grown. Brooks then argued that Clemens suffered extreme guilt feelings for having sold his artistic integrity and thus was set in motion the controversy with DeVoto, after which critics tended to echo much the same line regarding *What Is Man?* That is, its pessimism stemmed from personal motives, along with the *obiter dictum* that it revealed a lack of philosophic insight and style.

The "black despair" that DeVoto foisted on Clemens's last fifteen years actually lasted between two and three years after 1895. At least on October 7, 1898, Mrs. Clemens wrote in a letter, "I have not known Mr. Clemens to write with so much pleasure and energy as he has done the last summer."[37] Though it was published in *Harper's magazine* in December 1899, "The Man That Corrupted Hadleyburg" had been written more than a year earlier. Doubtlessly Twain's rejuvenated state had its effect on the quality of "Hadleyburg," which Kahn describes as "a masterpiece of construction and concentration: it moves swiftly, straight to the mark, without a wasted word."[38] A far cry from previous descriptions of this late work, which under DeVoto's pervasive influence tended to receive only "passing attention as a cynical and pessimistic story reflecting the deepening despair" of his last years.[39] Before DeVoto, Paine called it "one of the mightiest sermons against self-righteousness ever preached."[40] Paul J. Carter, Jr. ranks it near the top in power, second only to another moral fable of the same period, the "pathetic little story 'Was It Heaven?--or Hell.'"[41]

Through the Richardses, Twain reveals in "Hadleyburg" evidence of the determinism of <u>What Is Man</u>?, including the fundamental inconsistency noted earlier in the coexistence of unmistakable affirmation. The "despair" in the story is only evident if one perceives the village as representing the best of the race of mankind, because as Mary Richards accurately predicts early in the story,

> . . . it is my belief that this town's honesty is as rotten as mine is; as rotten as yours [her husband's] is. It is a mean town, a hard stingy town, and hasn't a virtue in the world but this honesty it is so celebrated for and so conceited about; and so help me, I do believe that if ever the day comes that its honesty falls under great temptation, its grand reputation will go to ruin like a house of cards.[42]

The determinism is evident in Mary's explanation of how Hadleyburg came to be as it is--through "training."

> . . . it's been one everlasting training and training and training in honesty--(but) honesty shielded, from the very cradle, against every possible temptation, and so it's artificial honesty, as weak as water when temptation comes. . . .[43]

Thus in the doctrine of What Is Man?, the Richardses like other Hadleyburgians had been trained, but trained "downward." The training is "artificial" and so will not hold up when temptation comes. But the point is not despair, for what the Hadleyburgians learn is finally affirmative, and the remainder of the story focuses upon the moral rebirth of Hadleyburg, the awakening of its moral perceptions that activate the conscience of the townspeople.

In short, Richards' training in the celebrated honesty of Hadleyburg has never been subjected to temptation or tested in the fires of experience, so that his conscience is like the Inner Master described in What Is Man? It seeks self-approval, being motivated by the desire for the good opinion of the town. Thus, as Paul Baender points out, Richards illustrates to perfection the Twainian gospel that conscience is "the sole impulse which dictates and compels a man's every act: the imperious necessity of securing his own approval, in every emergency and at all costs."[44] Indeed, Richards's desire for self-approval reflects his Hadleyburg training that has made "the reputation for honesty, the public image of the town . . . an obsession."[45] Yet Richards reveals that his "training" sensitizes his conscience, a sign that he may not continue to be a slave to public opinion. So the ironclad pessimism and despair of the later years is not quite so invulnerable as some critics have claimed. Such an examination of Twain's "gospel" indicates that "the saturnine determinist of What Is Man? left an opening for self-interest to guide itself toward society's welfare,"[46] Budd has pointed out, and thus undermines the sermon implied in the man-machine metaphor. In short, the elder Mark Twain, for all his reputation as a bleak pessimist, never relinquished a gut feeling that man can mend his ways and "train his ideals upward, and ever upward" until they satisfy both himself and his community. No matter that the fuzzy-minded philosopher at the beginning and end of What Is Man? had preached about man as a mere machine. The elder Twain would continue to sound the latter note stridently and often, so often as to lull critics into speaking of his "ultimate negation" and "nihilism."[47] Just as he would continue the role of the week-day preacher. In short, he never ceased to feel that reform was possible, as he demonstrated by carrying on "crusades" to the end of his days, as if designed to further the Old Man's plan for human betterment.[48] Intellectually, Mark Twain may have been a determinist, but emotionally, he remained the affirmer who preached at mankind through his humor and satire.

Nor have critics coming after DeVoto and Hill found the artistic failure and personal despair evident in Twain's later work. Tuckey's Mark Twain's Which Was the Dream? presents unpublished material written between 1896 and 1905 bound together by the theme of the "dream of failure"--even so, Tuckey is careful to present the evidence for a "balanced" state of mind. He notes, for instance, that "The last part of 'The Great Dar,' as written, expresses strength and hope, rather than futility and despair."[49] And of "Three Thousand Years Among the Microbes" he says, "This story, like other selections in this volume, was written with pleasure but written nevertheless under the shadow of disaster."[50]

But what Hamlin Hill refers to as "the junkyard of unfinished manuscripts and ill-conceived literary ideas" which Hill claims is "enduring testimony of the failure of Mark Twain to retain creative control over his world" is another matter.[51] It is true that Twain's concern with the dream as a central device and possible philosophical theme led him nowhere. Tuckey notes that behind Twain's "naive query" of whether reality was dream or vice versa "was his strong interest in conscious and unconscious levels of mental experience, which were then being explored by the new psychology."[52] Twain was, Tuckey says, "particularly interested in the relationship of the conscious and the unconscious levels of the mind, which he personified as the waking self and the dream self."[53] The material in <u>Mark Twain's Which Was the Dream?</u> is not artistically the best from this period of Twain's life, perhaps the equivalent in merit to the Huck and Tom material of the late eighties and early nineties-- <u>Tom Sawyer</u>, <u>Detective</u>; <u>Tom Sawyer Abroad</u>. But the material inspired by dream and/or that Twain attempted to shape by the dream represents only a part of his writing after 1896 and a part that as Macnaughton points out he put aside unfinished in 1902; "So ends," Macnaughton says, "the writer's involvement with a basic idea--the dream as disaster--that, for the numerous reasons already discussed, led to more false starts, literarily unproductive time, and bad writing than any other idea that caught Clemens's fancy during these last years."[54]

But as Macnaughton demonstrates, "One of the most remarkable and creative periods in Clemens's long career" was that between 1904 and 1906. After listing the material written, much of it published at the time, Macnaughton notes that "Much of this material is skillfully written; and some, though unfinished, is memorable and powerful."[55] Indeed, throughout his *Mark Twain's Last Years As a Writer*, Macnaughton carefully examines the artistry and skill Twain displayed at the end of his career. He shows how capable Twain remained as a writer and he explains why at various times in this period Twain did not or "could not write good, long fiction."[56] But Macnaughton is more than impressed with Twain's achievements in the last part of his life.

Maxwell Geismar has gone farther in his claims for the works of Twain's late years: ". . . Mark Twain not only survived and surmounted life's worst things, but . . . his later work far surpassed his earlier in knowledge and insight, in its range and complexity of artistic vision. It too is a celebration of life but with all its tragic depths; much more aware and complex than the rather simplistic innocence of Huck and Tom."[57] Far from seeing Twain's final years as artistically unproductive, Geismar goes so far as to say that "Even in fiction one might put *The Mysterious Stranger* in the same literary category as *Huck Finn*."[58] Though it may be difficult to agree with Geismar's assessment of either *Huck* or *The Mysterious Stranger*, it is impossible not to find great literary artistry in Twain's last years, in <u>The Mysterious Stranger</u>, <u>Letters from the Earth</u>, in the <u>Autobiography</u>, and not to agree with Geismar that

> Just in terms of prose style, Clemens's writing was never more eloquent and acute than in the radical phase of his later social criticism. There was . . . an abundant and delightful amplification, clarification, and impact. . . . And how much of it can you read without bursting into laughter?[59]

If in places Twain rages against the human race, its cowardice, its greed, its lack of intelligence, we should, first of all agree with him. Any reader of a major daily city newspaper in the U.S. must agree. But such a reader will also agree with Twain when elsewhere in his text he qualifies his universal damnation. If man is a coward, he is only partially so or occasionally so: "It is curious . . . that physical courage should be so common in the world, and moral courage so rare."[60] If physical courage is common, man obviously isn't commonly cowardly in many respects. In a letter to his friend Twichell in 1905, Clemens writes, "When a person is disloyal to any confessed duty, he is plainly and simply dishonest, and knows it; knows it, and is privately troubled about it and not proud of himself."[61] Thus man clearly has a conscience urging loyalty to duty, an attribute, to use Clemens's own terms, quite "creditable" in man. He continues in his letter to say, "Judged by this standard . . . there isn't an honest man in Connecticut, nor in the Senate, nor anywhere else. . . . For I know the human race's limitations . . . Each person in it is honest in one or several ways, but no member of it is honest in all ways required by--by what? <u>By his</u>

own standard."[62] No one could argue with Clemens's refusal to grant mankind absolute honesty. There is no pessimism, no nihilism here, only a recognition of humanity wanting to be good or honest in all the ways required by its own standards and a recognition of human failure. If anything, Clemens here gives man a far from despairing set of ideals to work from.

Clemens recognized clearly human complexity--virtue and vice in the same person. "Every man is a master and also a servant, a vassal," and " We are all alike--on the inside," he says in 1906.[63] But an example of almost any Twain "eruption" reveals contradictions. In his attack in 1906 on Thomas Reese, a man attempting to sell some of Twain's youthful writings, Clemens says,

> The common human trait which the Reeses have laid bare for inspection and which the rest of the nations of the earth carefully conceal for shame, and pretend that they do not possess, is the trait which urges a man to sacrifice all his pride, all his delicacy, all his decency, when his eye falls upon an unprotected dollar--a spectacle which sometimes takes the manhood out of him and leaves behind it nothing but the animal.[64]

Such a passage implies a Calvinistic selfishness that is held in check by reasoned virtues of pride, delicacy, and decency. Greed, the eye falling "upon an unprotected dollar," though it is a human trait, only "sometimes" deprives the race of its manhood. So if we are corrupt, we resist that inner corruption more times than not. What is noteworthy is that "the rest of the nations" or the greater part of mankind is able to conceal this universal human trait. Rather than praise the natural honesty of such people who do not conceal the trait, however, Twain simply notes that such people are a minority, a "breed." And they are "to be pitied, not reviled. They only obey the law of their nature. They did not make their nature; they are not responsible; and no humane person will permit himself to say harsh things about them."[65] Not peculiarly, Clemens contradicts his entire indictment of man by continuing a few lines later to say such people "dig up dead reputations and sell the rotten product for food, and eat the food. . . . which is another way of saying they fed upon the dead."[66] Once again, Clemens is trying to have it both ways. Man is corrupt and is in no way at fault for his corruption and those people who show the corruption are certainly beneath contempt, because they obviously are not responsible. In his attack on Bret Harte in 1907, Clemens says quite clearly, "He was bad, distinctly bad; he had no feeling, and he had no conscience."[67] Harte, Twain says, went to Europe and left his wife and "his little children behind, and never came back again from that time until his death, twenty-six years later."[68] Twain is evidently condemning Harte's "make," his lack of feeling and conscience, but he further condemns his lack of responsibility for those who should be close to him. None of this makes any sense, of course, if a man cannot help what he is, if his life is a succession of "accidents."

Twain later in 1908 recounting an interview with Elinor Glyn, says, "The fact is, she was brought up just like the rest of the world, with the ingrained and stupid superstition that there is such a thing as duty for duty's sake, . . . She believed that when a man held a private unpleasant opinion of an educational sort, which would get him hanged if he published it, he ought to publish it anyway and was a coward if he didn't. Take it all around, it was a very pleasant conversation. . . ."[69]

Twain's condemnation of Harte is partially over Harte's refusal to perform "duty for duty's sake," something Elinor Glyn is so immature as to believe. This "superstition" is obviously one that Twain himself shares--which is why he finds the conversation "very pleasant." He obviously likes hearing his own "superstitions." Twain used the word "superstition" about some of his own beliefs, his determinism, for instance: "According to this superstition of mine, the breaking of the toy is fully as important an event as the destruction of the throne, since without the breaking of the toy the destruction of the throne would not have happened."[70]

We see Twain pleased when his affirmative "superstition" is given to him from the mouth of another. In his 1908 interview with Elinor Glyn he records telling her that he regarded "the law of Nature . . . as the highest of laws, the most peremptory and absolute of all laws--Nature's laws being in my belief plainly and simply the laws of God, since He instituted them, He and no other. . . ."[71] People obeying such laws, such as the "indelicate" lovers in Glyn's novel Three Weeks, "were obeying the law of their make and disposition" and "therefore they were obeying the clearly enunciated law of God, and in his eyes must manifestly be blameless." But Clemens cannot "publicly" support such behavior, such "indelicacy":

> I said we were the servants of convention; that we could not subsist, either in a savage or a civilized state, without conventions; that we must accept them and stand by them, even when we disapproved of them; that while the laws of Nature, that is to say the laws of God, plainly make every human being a law unto himself, we must steadfastly refuse to obey those laws, and we must as steadfastly stand by the conventions which ignore them, since the statutes furnish us peace, fairly good government, and stability, and therefore are better for us than the laws of God, which would soon plunge us into confusion and disorder and anarchy, if we should adopt them.[72]

The argument here for the conventions existing in 1908, conventions that "furnish . . . peace, fairly good government, and stability," is far from pessimistic, nihilistic, or despairing. Even though it recognizes an innate conflict between natural and civilized, between private and public man, such recognition is not from a "new Mark Twain" in despair. DeVoto attributes a date of about 1886 to Twain's written comment, "The world loses a good deal by the laws of decorum; gains a good deal, of course, but certainly loses a good deal."[73] When Clemens refers to Executive Order 78, which he saw as an attempt to buy votes by extending the pension lists for disabled soldiers, he observed that "Everybody laughs--privately; everybody scoffs--privately; everybody is indignant--privately; everybody is ashamed to look a real soldier in the face--but none of them exposes his feelings publicly. This is perfectly natural, and wholly inevitable, for it is the nature of man to hate to say the disagreeable thing."[74] This commentary on man at least recognizes an inner virtue seemingly genuine in "everybody." Perhaps hating to say the disagreeable thing is decorum and moral courage is what has been lost in the necessary acquisition of decorum. Whatever the reasons and whatever the degree, Clemens is not totally pessimistic, not totally despairing of mankind, only occasionally and with qualification.

Finally, if Clemens is so despairing of man in this bitter period of his life, why in 1904, the very year of Livy's death, does he write, not just in praise of man but in praise of civilization, which is a point on which he is supposedly totally pessimistic:

> The valuable part--to my thinking the valuable part--of what we call civilization had no existence when she [Queen Victoria] emerged upon the planet. . . . She saw the whole of the new creation . . . A very creditable creation indeed, taking all things into account; since man, quite unassisted, did it all out of his own head. I jump to this conclusion because I think that if Providence had been minded to help him, it would have occurred to Providence to do this some hundred thousand centuries earlier. . . . We have been prompt to give Providence the credit of this fine and showy new civilization and we have been quite intemperate in our praises of this great benefaction; we have not been able to keep still over this splendid five minute attention; we can only keep still about the ages of neglect which preceded it and which it makes so conspicuous.[75]

Civilization here is "a very creditable creation," a "fine and showy new civilization," and credit for it goes to "man" who "unassisted did it all out of his own head."

And if in 1907, Clemens predicts the collapse of civilization and the return of "monarchy," he says, "a moral and mental midnight will follow--with a dull long sleep and a slow reawakening."[76] If there is a collapse, a "moral and mental midnight," there is still to be a "reawakening." If Twain is in despair over the present and future of civilization why do we not see the despair in 1906 in his comments on his purpose in A Connecticut Yankee, which Twain says, was "to contrast . . . the English life of the whole of the Middle Ages, with the life of modern Christendom and modern civilization--to the advantage of the latter, of course. That advantage is still claimable and does creditably and handsomely exist everywhere in Christendom-- if we leave out Russia and the royal palace of Belgium."[77] Even if Clemens is wrong about what a reader infers about his purpose, it is clear that in 1906 he thinks there is no question ("of course") about the "creditably and handsomely" existing advantage of modern civilization.

Continuing his attack on "the royal palace of Belgium"-- King Leopold II, Clemens observes, "It is curious that the most advanced and most enlightened century of all the centuries the sun has looked upon should have the ghastly distinction of having produced this moldy and piety-mouthing hypocrite, this bloody monster whose mate is not findable in human history anywhere, and whose personality will surely shame hell itself when he arrives there--which will be soon, let us hope and trust."[78] Not only is the present described as "the most advanced and most enlightened century" ever, Clemens is far from pessimistic in hoping and trusting Leopold will soon cease his evil acts.

Many if not most of Clemens's pessimistic attacks on man,

civilization, the U.S. government, are undercut by optimism. In a letter to Howells in 1900 on the Boer War Clemens writes:

> Privately speaking, this is a sordid and criminal war . . . England must not fall; it would mean an inundation of Russian and German political degradations which would envelope the globe and steep it in a sort of Middle-Age night and slavery which would last till Christ comes again. Even wrong--and she is wrong--England must be upheld. He is an enemy of the human race who shall speak against her now. Why <u>was</u> the human created? Or at least why wasn't something creditable created in place of it. God had his opportunity. He could have made a reputation. But no, He must commit this grotesque folly--a lark which must have cost him a regret or two when He came to think it over and observe effects. . . . Then I say "My head is with the Briton, but my heart and such rags of morals as I have are with the Boer--"[79]

The human race is not "creditable," is a "grotesque folly," yet Clemens is clearly not its "enemy." Furthermore, Clemens recognizes the conflicting loyalties of head and heart in himself, and in mankind. His realistic observation that human kind is an amalgam of emotions, virtues, vices must argue against any sort of overly simplistic pessimistic or nihilistic view of man.

In a 1905 letter to Twichell about Roosevelt, Clemens observes, "we are all insane, each in his own way, and with insanity goes irresponsibility. Theodore the man is sane; in fairness we ought to keep in mind that Theodore, as statesman and politician, is insane and irresponsible."[80] At several points in his late work, Clemens comments on everyone being only temporarily sane, human personality being anything other than stable. In February of 1906, recording Olivia's nursing a friend with typhoid fever in the Clemens household in the early years of their marriage, Clemens writes, "Those two or three days are among the blackest, the gloomiest, the most wretched of my long life. The resulting periodical and sudden changes of mood in me, from deep melancholy to half-insane tempests and cyclones of humor, are among the curiosities of my life."[81] Among the blackest days of his long life are some spent in the early years of his marriage; Clemens doesn't argue here for his last ten years being the blackest. He further recognizes in himself swift shifts of mood, implying an incapacity for sustaining melancholy even in the blackest days of it.

Of himself and man in general, Clemens wrote to Reverend L. M. Powers in 1905, "Pessimists are born not made; optimists are born not made; but no man is born either pessimist wholly or optimist wholly, perhaps; he is pessimistic along certain lines and optimistic along certain others. That is my case."[82] This realistic instability was commented upon by his biographer Paine, "In much of his later writing . . . and certainly in his purely intellectually moments he was likely to be pessimist of the most extreme type, capably damning the race and the inventor of it. Yet, at heart, no man loved his kind more genuinely, or with deeper compassion, than Mark Twain, perhaps for its very weaknesses."[83]

Clemens's daughter Clara made the very same observation,

> To him the human race was irretrievably bad . . . but in the very next moment, if some caller entered and recounted an incident picturing the noble conduct of a mother, husband, child, his eyes would fill with tears and he would pace the floor, exclaiming: "What noble generosity! By gosh! that's a fine man for you!"

Fortunately, his heart was fully as strong as his head.[84]

The more than simple division of head and heart is evident in Clemens's scheme "to write letters to friends & not send them" as a means of getting by the restraints posed in dictating his autobiography to a stenographer: "When you are on fire with theology, you'll not write it to Rogers, who wouldn't be an inspiration, you'll write it to Twichell, because it would make him writhe & squirm & break the furniture. When you are on fire with a good thing that's indecent, you won't waste it on Twichell, you'll save it for Howells, who will love it."[85]

It is time to put away the myth of a "new Twain" despairing pessimistic, nihilistic, a product of the many "tragedies" that befell him prior to the last ten years of his life. According to A. B. Paine, Clemens's "poverty and debt" became acute about the beginning of 1895.[86] Eleven years later, in February, 1906 when Clemens talks of Livy being dead now "one year and eight months," he says that "during the nine years that we spent in poverty and debt she was always able to reason me out of my despairs and find a bright side to the clouds and make me see it."[87] If Clemens is being honest here, any permanent despair had to occur after Livy's death in 1904, since she was "always" able to make him see "a bright side." Anyone looking at Clemens's letters and writing after the death of his wife in 1904 will find anger, pessimism and despair, the very same anger, pessimism and despair evident before 1900, and the very same wit, love, enthusiasm, and appreciation for this world.

Clemens remained interested in his work after Livy's death. He writes to Duneka in July, 1905 about a current project: "Adam's Diary is dam good," and again in October, "I have just finished a short story which I 'greatly admire,'" and so will you-- . . . It has good fun in it, and several characters, and is lively. . . ."[88] In 1906, Clemens says, "There has never been a time in the past thirty-five years when my literary shipyard hadn't two or more half-finished ships on the ways, neglected and baking in the sun; generally there have been three or four; at present there are five."[89] So, in his seventies he has one or more unfinished manuscripts than "generally" in the past thirty-five years. In a letter to Howells in 1906, he says of his work on the autobiography, "I have such volumes and volumes of things that I want to say" that he will not need reminders of things to include in the work.[90] It is true that he writes Howells in August of 1908 that "I have retired from labor for good, I have dismissed my stenographer and have entered upon a holiday whose other end is in the cemetery," but in a letter of November 1909, he writes that "I've been writing "'Letters from the Earth.'"[91] Clearly Mark Twain was writing with vigor and effect throughout the last ten years of his life when he was supposedly in despair.

If the last ten years of his life were spent in despair, what did Clemens mean in January of 1906 in a letter to his friends, saying "I am old; I recognize it but I don't realize it. I wonder if a person ever really ceases to feel young--I mean, for a whole day at a time."[92] What did he mean in March of 1906 when he wrote, "Girls are charming creatures. I shall have to be twice seventy years old before I change my mind as to that. I am to talk to a crowd of them this afternoon, students of Barnard College . . . and I think I shall have just as pleasant a time with those lassies as I had with the Vassar girls twenty-one years ago."[93] What does he mean when he writes Emilie Rogers in October 1906, "The long railway journey from Dublin last Wednesday <u>destroyed</u> me for 7 whole days!--both mentally and physically; . . . Indeed, to use Uncle Henry's phrase, I've had a hell of a week. At last, the week culminated last night with an assault of a disease I am not much subject to--depression of spirits. But I am all right, this morning, in <u>all</u> ways."[94]

If he is nihilistic and pessimistic, why in 1906 does he say speaking in reference to an association being formed in the interests of the adult blind, ". . . I came away with the conviction that excellent enterprise is going to flourish, and will bear abundant fruit."[95] Why does he write to a Mrs. Whitmore in February of 1907, "the truth is that when a Library expels a book of mine and leaves an unexpurgated Bible lying around where unprotected youth and age can get hold of it, the deep unconscious irony of it delights me and doesn't anger me. But even if it angered me such words as those of Professor Phelps would take the sting all out."?[96] If he is in despair and delights in nothing, how can he write Howells in August of 1908, inviting him for a visit in "the most satisfactory house I am acquainted with, and the most satisfactorily situated. But it is no place to work in, because one is outside of it all the time, while the sun and the moon are on duty."[97] Why does he write again two months later, "Come along. This place seemed at its best when all around was summer-green; . . . and now once more it seems at its best, with the trees naked and the ground a painter's palette."? And three months later in January of 1909, "It is lively up here now. I wish you would come."?[98] And why as late as a few months before his death in November 1909 does he write a friend, "The autumn splendors pass you by? . . . I wish you had been here. It was beyond words! It was heaven and hell and sunset and rainbows and the aurora all fused into one divine harmony, and you couldn't look at it and keep the tears back. . . . I wish I could go on the platform and read. . . . There's a charity-school of 400 young girls in Boston that I would give my ears to talk to, if I had some more . . ."?[99] And the letters and reports go up to the very end--appreciating nature, friends, books, his own work.

In the accounts given by members of his family it is evident that Clemens alone attacks mankind and everyone else defends it --thus it was Twain against the world, wonderfully heroic odds for someone who wanted to be the center of attention and could hold center stage by ranting magnificently. And there was the core of truth in it all--every man capable of baseness, every man having to resist the lure of the dollar, every man afraid of society's ridicule; but if Clemens had found widespread agreement for his sometimes vituperative attacks on the human race, he would have quickly leaped to its defense. In 1906, Twain laments a lapse in "the political and commercial morals of the United States":

> Before Jay Gould's time there was a fine phrase . . . "The press is the palladium of our liberties." It was a serious saying and it was a true saying, but it is long ago dead and has been tucked safely away in the limbo of oblivion. No one would venture it now except as a sarcasm.[100]

What has provoked Clemens to this attack on the press is an article in the Denver Post on the recent election of Simon Guggenheim to the U. S. Senate: The article states, in part

> "Mr. Guggenheim . . . is just the man for the place. There is no use trying to reform the world. They have been trying that for two thousand years and haven't succeeded. Mr. Guggenheim is the choice of the people and they ought to have him, even if he spent a million dollars. The issue of the election was Tom Patterson and Simon Guggenheim, and the people chose Guggenheim. The Denver Post bows to the will of the people."[101]

Clemens is clearly outraged: "Mr. Guggenheim has lately been chosen United States Senator reputedly by a bought legislature in Colorado which is almost the customary way, now, of electing United States Senators," and, of course, it is only what is to be expected from "the human race," but Clemens's scorn here is for the press, specifically for the Denver Post, which is simply and clearly stating Twain's own pessimistic principle: "There is no use trying to reform the world. They have been trying that for two thousand years and haven't succeeded."[102] Why condemn the Post for acting on Twain's often spoken axiom? Because though Twain spoke the principle, Clemens didn't accept it. If he is sincere in his condemnation of the United States of Lyncherdom, why in 1907 condemn Bret Harte for not having "any more passion for his country than an oyster has for its bed"?[103]

Even if Twain is a determinist, nothing insists that he despair. In 1906, Twain summarizes a conversation (more a lecture, in fact) with a woman who thanks him for a favor he does her, a favor she sees as "ordered," ordered "By the Power that watches over us and commands all events." His lecture includes the following:

> I am not jesting. I have studied these things a long time and I positively believe that the first circumstance that ever happened in this world was the parent of every circumstance that has happened in this world since; that God ordered that first circumstance and has never ordered another one from that day to this. Plainly, then, I am not able to conceive of such a thing as the thing which we call an <u>accident</u>--that is to say, an event without a cause.[104]

Very clearly, Twain asserts here several noteworthy points. His point is that he believes in a determinism, a determinism initiated by "God"--whom Thomas Paine defines as "a first Cause eternally existing"--who since his first act has removed himself from the affairs of men and galaxies. Twain insists that he is not joking in stating this belief. Such a belief is entirely consistent with a rationalist's view of the world and in no way presupposes despair.

Some lines later in his lecture, Twain defines an "accident" as "a word which I constantly make use of when I am talking to myself about the chain of incidents which has constituted my life," and then proceeds to summarize his life through a series of "accidents" beginning at the age of six. This summary lasts for six pages and uses the word "accident" some twenty five times until Twain come to the "accident" of seeing Olivia Langdon's picture and later marrying her. At this point he says, "out of this happy accident resulted a thousand other happy accidents, link after link, year after year, until the chain reached down to you and your affairs, a week ago." Twain's brief summary of his life is couched in terms of simply "accident until he marries Livy, at which point the "accident" and his "life" are described as "happy" and his life and the accidents "a thousand other happy accidents" continue "link after link, year after year, until . . . a week ago."[105] This is certainly no description of a life lived in despair up until 1906. In 1907, Clemens cites the occasion of his first meeting with Livy, an event he says that "made the real fortune of my life in that it made the happiness of my life. . . . It was forty years ago; from that day to this [she] has never been out of my mind nor heart."[106] In December 1909 Clemens wrote to his daughter Clara upon the death of his daughter Jean, "I am so glad she is out of it and safe--safe! I am not melancholy; I shall never be melancholy again, I think."[107] Clemens's very last words to his daughter before he fell into the sleep in which he died, were "Goodbye dear, if we meet--" a fragment suggesting the lack of certainty, the incipient hope of love that typified his entire adult life, not a final ten years of despair.[108]

DeVoto's selections from the Autobiography in <u>Mark Twain in Eruption</u> containing Twain's fulminations against mankind and trivia are often just that--eruptions; and it is difficult to see a Samuel Clemens or anyone else despairing in the act of erupting. What DeVoto seemed not to understand and what seems quite evident in all of his autobiographical writings is that Twain enjoyed ranting. It was funny and he knew it, which does not mean that he wasn't being truthful at the core of his rant, but that to be funny he had to exaggerate, a small price to pay to achieve laughter--"that rare and precious pleasure."[109] Even in his diatribes the evoked laughter forces us to know that Twain wrote with enjoyment and pleasured in knowing he evoked laughter. His attack on Theodore Roosevelt is entirely too hilarious to be the work of anyone in despair, and other parts of the <u>Autobiography</u> and <u>Letters from the Earth</u> are as good as anything Twain ever wrote. The material from the last ten years of Clemens's life shows appreciation, delight, love for people, places, things, human behavior towards himself and others, and above all a continued vitality that belies both despair and artistic decline.

To be sure, Twain's negativism is ever likely to assert itself, even blatantly, in his crusading. His Swiftian rages were doubtless intensified by his life-long imperfect control over his temper and by his long-held habit of editorializing on the latest antics of humanity. Such comment stems from the same old sources. The Calvinism with its conviction of total and innate depravity, a damned human race, a race born of evil and into evil, with its same logical inconsistency of preaching hellfire and damnation to those who theoretically were born damned and who were powerless to achieve salvation since grace was given freely by god only to some and they completely undeserving. The Enlightenment thought that asserted the importance of the environment in providing the ideals to be imposed upon the tabula rasa that would "train . . . ever and ever upward" toward a worldly perfection utterly impossible in Calvinism. A Romanticism that asserted the destruction of a society warped by environment and demanding a return to a primordial goodness inherent in nature. Twain the romantic is Twain the revolutionist; Twain the Man of the Enlightenment accepts a morally structured world and draws his satirizing pen against those who distort the moral structure. Twain the Calvinist is convinced of the inherent evil in the world and, in self-loathing at his own unworthiness, lashes out at a damned universe, contradicting his own despair in his castigation of helpless victims.

And if Twain seems hopelessly confused as a philosopher in his contradictions, he is no more so than his contemporary American artists and thinkers. A Henry Adams who felt the world gone bad and looked to no good end, but still felt compelled to try and understand why, when it made no difference if it had truly gone bad. An Oliver Wendell Holmes, Jr. who asserted the necessity of struggle amidst the absence of certainty--to what end, one may ask. A William James who knew that nothing was knowable except what was immediate and that only until the sensation possibly changed it. A Santayana who saw the world as ugly and hostile and senseless and persisted in a cerebral quest for the aesthetic.

ENDNOTES TO CHAPTER VIII

1. Notebook, p. 256.
2. Bernard DeVoto, Mark Twain in Eruption (New York and London, Harper & Brothers, 1940) p. xix.
3. Mark Twain In Eruption, p. xix.
4. Mark Twain in Eruption, pp. xx-xxi.
5. Hamlin Hill, Mark Twain: God's Fool (New York, Harper & Row, 1973), pp. 272-273.
6. Hamlin Hill, p. 274.
7. John S. Tuckey, Mark Twain's Which Was the Dream? (Berkeley, University of California Press, 1967), pp. 1-2.
8. John S. Tuckey, p. 430.
9. Frederick, The Darkened Sky, p. 171.
10. Budd, Mark Twain: Social Philosopher, p. 169.
11. Edwin S. Fussell, "The Structural Problem of The Mysterious Stranger," reprinted in The Mysterious Stranger and the Critics, ed. John S. Tuckey (Belmont California: Wadsworth Publishing Co., Inc., 1968), 75-83 (p. 82).
12. John S. Tuckey, "Mark Twain's Later Dialogue: The 'Me' and the Machine," American Literature, 41 (January 1970), p. 532.
13. What Is Man? And Other Philosophical Writings, ed. Paul Baender (Berkeley, Los Angeles, London: University of California, 1973). p. 128.

14. *What Is Man*? p. 131.
15. *What Is Man*? p. 131.
16. *What Is Man*? p. 136.
17. *What Is Man*? p. 137.
18. *What Is Man*? p. 140.
19. *What Is Man*? p. 140-41, 206.
20. *What Is Man*? pp. 141, 142.
21. *What Is Man*? p. 156.
22. *What Is Man*? p. 161.
23. *What Is Man*? pp. 161-63.
24. *What Is Man*? pp. 163, 164, 165.
25. *What Is Man*? p. 165.
26. *What Is Man*? p. 170.
27. Jones, "Mark Twain and the Determinism of *What Is Man?* *American Literature*, Vol. 29, No. 1 (March 1957), 1-17 (p.15).
28. Paine, III, 1321-22.
29. Adams, *Everyman's Psychology* (Garden City, New York: Doubleday, Doran and Company, 1929), p. 204.
30. Flowers, "Mark Twain's Theories of Morality," Ph.D. dissertation, Louisiana State University, 1941), p. 487.
31. Baender, ed., *What Is Man*,? p. 13, note 25; Jones, "Mark Twain and the Determinism of *What Is Man*?," *American Literature*, 29 (March 1957), 1017 (p. 15).
32. Jones, "Determinism of *What Is Man*?," pp. 1, 7.
33. Baender, p. 17.

34. *New York Times Review of Books*, June 3, 1917, p. 216; see Baender, p. 19.
35. Horace James Bridges, "The Pessimism of Mark Twain," published in the *Standard* (Cooperstown, New York), July 1919, and reprinted in Bridges' *As I Was Saying* (Boston: Marshall Jones, 1923), pp. 35-51.
36. *Our America* (New York: Boni and Liveright, 1919), p. 43.
37. Kahn, *Mark Twain's Mysterious Stranger: A Study of the Manuscript Text*, p. 44.
38. Kahn, p. 44.
39. Clinton B. Burhaus, Jr., "The Sober Affirmation of Mark Twain's Hadleyburg," *American Literature*, Vol. 34 (Nov. 1962), 375-384 (p. 375).
40. Paine, II, 1069.
41. Carter, "Mark Twain" Moralist in Disguise," *University of Colorado Studies in Language and Literature*, Vol. 6 (January 1957), 65-79 (p. 72, Note 26).
42. "*The Man That Corrupted Hadleyburg*" And Other Essays And Stories." Stormfield Edition, Vol. XXIII (New York and London: Harper & Brothers, 1929), pp. 15-16.
43. "*Hadleyburg*," p. 15.
44. *What Is Man*?, p. 147.
45. Burhaus, "The Sober Affirmation," p. 379, Note 8.
46. Budd, *Mark Twain: Social Philosopher*, p. 206.
47. Frederick, *The Darkened Sky*, pp. 147, 172.
48. Budd speaks of the "latter-day Twain as a 'crusader,'"

Social Philosopher, p. 207.

49. Tuckey, p. 19.
50. Tuckey, p. 430.
51. Hamlih Hill, p. 273.
52. Tuckey, p. 2.
53. Tuckey, p. 17.
54. William R. Macnaughton, Mark Twain's Last Years as a Writer, pp. 188-89.
55. Macnaughton, pp. 202, 203.
56. Macnaughton, p. 167.
57. Maxwell Grismar, Mark Twain: An American Prophet (Boston, Houghton Mifflin, 1970), p. 442.
58. Geismar, p. 442.
59. Geismar, p. 480.
60. Mark Twain in Eruption, p. 69.
61. Albert Bigelow Paine, Mark Twain's Letters Vol 2 (New York and London, 1929), p. 768.
62. Letters Vol. 2, p. 768.
63. Mark Twain in Eruption, pp. 67, 46.
64. Eruption, p. 238.
65. Eruption, p. 238.
66. Eruption, p. 238-39.
67. Eruption, p. 272.
68. Eruption, p. 272.
69. Eruption, p. 318.
70. Eruption, p. 386.

71. *Eruption*, p. 315.
72. *Eruption*, p. 315-16.
73. *Eruption*, p. 366.
74. *Eruption*, p. 70.
75. Albert Bigelow Paine, ed., *Mark Twain's Autobiography*, Vol. I (New York and London, Harper & Brothers, 1929), pp. 208-09.
76. *Eruption*, p. 67.
77. *Eruption*, p. 211.
78. *Eruption*, p. 212.
79. *Letters*, Vol. 2, p. 693.
80. *Letters*, Vol. 2, p. 767.
81. *Eruption*, p. 251.
82. *Letters*, Vol.2, p. 785.
83. *Letters*, Vol. 2, p. 767.
84. Clara Clemens, *My Father: Mark Twain*, (New York and London, Harper & Brothers, 1931), p. 182.
85. Frederick Anderson, William M. Gibson, Henry Nash Smith, eds., *Selected Mark Twain-Howells Letters* (Cambridge, The Belknap Press of Harvard University Press, 1967), pp, 402-03.
86. *Letters*, Vol. 2, p. 27.
87. *Autobiography*, Vol. II, P. 27.
88. *Letters*, Vol. 2, pp. 775, 778.
89. *Eruption*, p. 196.
90. *Selected Mark Twain-Howells Letters*, p. 807.

91. *Letters*, Vol. 2, pp. 816-17, 833.

92. *Letters*, Vol. 2, p. 789.

93. *Autobiography*, Vol. II, p. 172.

94. Lewis Leary, ed., *Mark Twain's Correspondence with Henry Huttleston Rogers*, (Berkeley and Los Angeles, University of California Press, 1969), p. 618.

95. *Autobiography*, Vol. II, pp. 295-96.

96. *Letters*, Vol. 2, p. 805.

97. *Letters*, Vol. 2, p. 816.

98. *Letters*, Vol. 2, p. 830.

99. *Letters*, Vol. 2, p. 834.

100. *Eruption*, p. 81.

101. *Eruption*, p. 82.

102. *Eruption*, p. 82.

103. *Eruption*, p. 286.

104. *Eruption*, p. 386.

105. *Eruption*, p. 392-93.

106. *Eruption*, p. 213.

107. *Letters*, Vol. 2, p. 835.

108. *My Father: Mark Twain*, p. 291.

109. *Eruption*, p. 118.

CHAPTER IX: CONCLUSION

The idea that Samuel Clemens grew increasingly bitter in his later years and ended his life in despair of man, god, and the universe is a myth of long standing. Unfortunately, it is also a myth that leads to a misunderstanding of the man and his works, a myth derived from selective evidence that portrays Mark Twain as a comic genius of sophomoric temperament and marginal intellectual powers. In truth, an examination of many of the very works providing evidence of despair reveals that Samuel Clemens had a much more complicated view of the universe. His very inability to embrace a particular philosophical system that could have led him to a bitter despair or a shallow optimism is revealed in his life and his work and shows a spiritual integrity that reflects opposing religious thoughts promulgated throughout the American experience.

Samuel Clemens's childhood in Hannibal, Missouri exposed him to a variety of religious concepts, most of them deriving from offshoots of Calvinism but including the supernaturalism of slaves, a spiritualism of nineteenth century enthusiasts, and a rational skepticism. While there is no indication that he practiced anything other than orthodoxy in his boyhood, shortly after leaving Hannibal, Clemens was clearly and powerfully exposed to the Enlightenment ideas of Thomas Paine, ideas incompatible with Calvinism. Though Twain cannot be said to have abandoned all of the principles or nuances of Calvinism, <u>Innocents Abroad</u>, and some of his other early work shows a shift from Calvinistic to Deistic views. Later work, such as <u>Tom Sawyer</u>, shows that Twain developed an even more complex view of the universe and man, a view that embraces values more akin to Romanticism than to either Calvinism or the rationalism of the Enlightenment. Finally, the scientific determinism--incorporating characteristics of both Calvinism and rationalism--of his own times exerted an influence apparent in the works of his middle and later years.

The conflicting views of man as sinful or good or neither but capable of becoming either and views of god and the universe as benevolent, hostile, or indifferent are all evident in Twain's masterpiece, <u>Huckleberry Finn</u>, a masterpiece in part because these conflicting views provide a lack of philosophical resolution in keeping with the reality of American experience. These same opposing systems are inherent in our culture today. But Clemens's refusal finally to accept a single system is, if anything, a realistic confusion. It is not despair. If Twain saw the human race as damned on one page, he found hope for the race on the next page. His later extended works and his comments show the same indecision, the same lack of resolution to the crucial questions of the nature of god, man, and the universe.

What finally comes through about Clemens is not that he is a bad, inconsistent thinker, but that he is a complex thinker, comprising within himself the totality of confused American thought and culture, as his *Huckleberry Finn* is a compendium of the American experience from the frontier of Plymouth and Jamestown to the end of the nineteenth century. In this persistent confusion over conflicting of ways of seeing the world--liberal, Romantic, man is good, the universe wonderful, god is on our side vs. conservative, Calvinistic, man is bad, the universe is the devil's workshop, god is on our side but we don't deserve it--lies Samuel Clemens's understanding of man, perhaps best expressed in the words of Mrs. Richards in "The Man That Corrupted Hadleyburg": "Lord, how strangely we are made," and in the ultimate moral of that tale's conclusion, "Lead Us Into Temptation." Nothing else in the late Twain verifies more clearly the substance of *Huckleberry Finn*, Twain's highest achievement acknowledging the infinite complexity, perversity, and unknowableness of the human spirit's blessed contradictoriness in a baffling universe presided over or perhaps within a great unknown.

INDEX

Adams, Henry, 167, 210
Adams, Sir John, 186
Age of Reason, The, 20, 21, 22, 24, 48, 59, 76, 80, 101, 107
Agnosticism, 17
Arthur, King, 152ff
Autobiography of Mark Twain, The, 179, 193
Baender, Paul, 22, 168, 189
Barnes, George E., 74
Beard, Charles, 72
Beecher, Henry Ward, 57
Behaviroism, 110
Bell, Millicent, 145
Bellamy, Gladys, 22, 30
Blaine, James G., 114
Blair, Walter, 86, 100, 130
Boer War, 200
Bounty, the sailing ship, 99
Branch, Edgar M., 29, 126
Brashear, Minnie, 4, 9, 20
Brooks, Van Wyck, 1, 2, 3, 4, 5, 56, 179
Budd, Louis, 100, 144, 181
Bulletin, the San Francisco, 32
Burrough, Frank E., 19
Call, the San Francisco, 74
Calvinism, 1, 4, 5, 7, 10, 11, 17, 27, 33, 38, 43, 47, 78, 79, 80, 87ff, 95, 103, 107, 113, 121, 126, 132, 137, 139, 140, 141, 155, 182, 219-221
Campbell, Alexander, 6, 7, 8, 9, 30, 133
Caples, 8
"Captain Stormfield's Visit to Heaven," 59
Carnege, Andrew, 186
Carter, Paul R., Jr., 188
Catholicism, 19, 44-47, 154
"Character of Man, The," 114, 115, 124
Christian Science, 163
"Chronicle of Young Satan, The," 164
Clemens, Clara, 158, 201, 208
Clemens, Cyril, 4
Clemens, Henry, 21, 22
Clemens, Jane, 4, 5, 7
Clemens, Jean, 113
Clemens, John Marshall, 7, 18, 21
Clemens, Olivia Langdon, 43, 56-60, 200, 202, 208
Clemens, Orion, 19, 23, 26
Clemens, Pamela, 5
Connecticut Yankee in King Arthur's Court, A, 145, 151-167, 199
Courier, the Hannibal, 8, 9

Curious Republick of Gondour and Other Whimsical Sketches, The, 65
Daily Journal, the Hannibal, 19
Darwin, Charles, 76
Deism, 8, 20, 24, 25, 26, 31, 48, 99, 101, 103, 107, 111, 121, 181, 220
Democracy, 167
Determinism, 12, 80, 109, 113, 121, 153, 220
DeVoto, Bernard, 2, 3, 9, 18, 85, 123, 151, 179, 188, 190, 197
"Disgraceful Persecution of a Boy," 34, 74-75
Duneka, Frederick, 3, 203
"Dutch Nick Massacre, The," 26
Eddy, Mary Baker, 163
Edwards, Johnathan, 95
Egan, Michael, 143, 144
Enlightenment, the, 59
Elijah, 98
"Facts Concerning the Recent Carnival of Crime in Connecticut," 92-94, 129
"First Class in Modern Moral Philosophy," 66, 67
Flowers, Frank C., 186
Frank, Waldo, 187
Franklin, Benjamin, 129
Frederick, John T., 4, 112, 151
Freemasonary, 24, 25, 48
Galaxy Magazine, 28, 34, 74
Geismar, Maxwell, 85, 90, 94, 95, 192, 193
Gilded Age, The, 65, 67-72, 80, 99, 134, 136
Gillis, Steve, 34
Glyn, Elinor, 195, 196
"Great Revolution in Pitcairn, The," 99-101
Gould, Jay, 70, 206
Gross, Seymour, 113
Guggenheim, Simon, 206
Haeckel, Ernst Heinrich, 76
Hall, New York Mayor A. Oakley, 66
Hart, Bernard, 2
Harte, Bret, 195, 207
Hartford Monday Evening Club, 108, 153
Hazard of New Fortunes, A, 167
Hill, Hamlin, 180, 191
Holland, George, 73
Holmes, Oliver Wendell, Jr., 210
Hopson, Elder, 8
Howell,s William Dean, 110, 111, 167, 202-205
Huckleberry Finn, Adventures of, 85, 112, 121-147, 151, 164, 220, 221
Huxley, Thomas Henry, 76
Innocents Abroad, The, 43-55, 65, 69, 220
James, William, 212
Janes, The Rev. Bishop, 65
Joan of Arc, Personal Recollections of, 151, 172-175

Jones, Alexander E., 4, 24, 186
Journal, the Hannibal, 8
Kaplan, Justin, 4, 11, 69, 112, 162, 163
Know, Nothingism, 69
League, Bill, 6
Letters from the Earth, 193
Leopold II, Belgian King, 199
Lynn, Kenneth S., 43, 93, 94
Macnaughton, William R., 163, 191
McCormick, Wales, 8, 9
"Man That Corrupted Hadleyburg, The," 28, 187ff, 221
Manford, The Rev. Mr. E., 8
Manifest Destiny, 3
Mark Twain's America, 2
Mark Twain At Work, 3
Mark Twain: Business Man, 4
Mark Twain's Last Years as a Writer, 192
Mark Twain's Which Was the Dream?, 180, 190, 191
Martin, Jay, 144
Marx, Leo, 144
Melville, Herman, 89
Methodism, 5, 18, 30
Miller, William [also Millerite], 6, 7
Moses, 23
Mr. Clemens and Mark Twain, 4
Mysterious Stranger, The, 3, 164-166, 181, 192, 193
Nihilism, 4, 204
"Open Letter to Commodore Vanderbilt," 65, 66
Packard Monthly, 65
Paine, Albert B., 1, 3, 4, 17, 20, 21, 22, 27, 59, 60, 109, 110, 188, 202
Paine, Thomas, 20, 22, 26, 59, 80, 101, 107, 207, 219
Pennsylvania, the steamboat, 21
Pike, Albert, 24
Post, the Denver, 206
Powers, the Rev. Mr. L. M., 203
Predestination, 8
Prelapsarianism, 88
Presbyterianism, 5, 7, 10, 17, 18, 31, 32, 48, 97, 111, 132, 159
"Private History of a Campaign that Failed, The," 162
Psychology of Insanity, The, 2
Pudd'nhead Wilson, 151, 166-172
Quaker City, the steamship, 43, 47, 57
Quarles, John, 7, 8, 111, 181
Rank, Otto, 94
Rationalism, 12, 38, 45, 51, 95, 101, 121, 220
"Reflections on the Sabbath," 32, 33
Rogers, Emilie, 204
Rogers, H. H., 202
Romanticism, 12, 80, 85, 96, 121, 220
Roosevelt, Theodore, 209
Ruffner, Betty, 6

Rush, the Rev. Mr. W. M., 8
Sabine, the Rev. Mr. William T., 73
Santayana, George, 213
Smith, Henry Nash, 33, 85, 86, 124, 151, 169
Socrates, 48
Solomon, Roger, 173, 174
"Some Learned Fables for Good Old Boys and Girls," 65, 77-80
"Some Rambling Notes," 96-98
"Song of Myself, " 120
Spiritualism, 6, 7, 17, 29, 30, 32
Stewart, Bill, 26
Stoddard, Charles Warner, 112, 113
"Story of a Bad Little Boy That Bore a Charmed Life, The," 28
"Stories for Good Little Boys and Girls," 28
"Story of a Good Little Boy Who Did Not Prosper, The," 28
Strout, Cushing 161, 162, 163
Talmage, the Rev. Mr. T. DeWitt, 72
Tammany Ring, 66
<u>Tom Sawyer, The Adventures of</u>, 79, 80, 85-92, 220
<u>Tom Sawyer Abroad</u>, 191
<u>Tom Sawyer, Detective</u>, 191
<u>Tribune</u>, the New York, 66, 69, 70
<u>Tri-Weekly Messenger</u>, the Hannibal, 6
<u>Tramp Abroad,A</u>, 102
<u>Troubled Heart, A,</u> 112
Tuckey, John S., 3, 180, 182, 190, 191
Tweed, "Boss" William M., 66, 67
Twichell, the Rev. Mr. Joseph, 60, 102, 193, 200, 202
<u>Union</u>, the Sacramento, 34
Universalism, 8, 10, 17, 183
Vanderbilt, Commodore Cornelius, 65, 66
<u>Veracious Imagination, The</u>, 161
"Villagers of 1840-43", 6
Wadsworth, the Rev. Mr. Charles, 29, 31
Warner, Charles Dudley, 65
Webster, Annie Moffett, 4, 23
Webster, Samuel Charles, 4
Wecter, Dixon, 4, 5, 7, 17, 58
<u>What Is Man?</u>, 109, 111, 113, 130, 179, 180, 182-190
"What Is Happiness?," 115
Whitman, Walt, 122
Whitmore, Mrs., 204
Wigger, Anne P., 171
Wiggins, Robert, 174

Benjamin Newman

SEARCHING FOR THE FIGURE IN THE CARPET IN THE TALES OF HENRY JAMES
Reflections of an Ordinary Reader

American University Studies: Series 4 (English Language and Literature).
Vol. 49
ISBN 0-8204-0442-X   200 pages   hardback $ 39.00/sFr. 59.00

Recommended prices – alterations reserved

Undertaken as if by an ordinary reader concentrating upon fundamentals of feeling and thought in the tales of Henry James, this study by Professor Newman is a probing, questioning, analytical search for the Jamesian figure, for the ultimate messages communicated by James about his life and the world. Joining this distinctive perspective, a personalized style, and solid scholarly exploration, the book probes for meaning behind visions and metaphors over an expanse from *Daisy Miller* to *The Jolly Corner*, from the early years to the closing stage, the final years of recollection. As the odyssey progresses, its findings confirm for the author his conviction that there is indeed a «figure in the carpet», a consistent, coherent, and unified vision of James's life and of man's that runs through the tales, but modified in certain ways as the years passed. It is a complex design which, once uncovered and grasped, enables the reader to penetrate James's symbolic system, to resolve the so-called ambiguities and obscurities so often ascribed to him, and to interpret with confidence what James is saying to us as he writes about life and society, about art and personal passion and death.

PETER LANG PUBLISHING, INC.
62 West 45th Street
USA – New York, NY 10036

Philip Freneau

TOMO CHEEKI, THE CREEK INDIAN PHILADELPHIA
Edited by Elisabeth Hermann

Studien und Texte zur Amerikanistik – Texte. Bd. 6
ISBN 3-8204-0105-9   123 pages   paperback $ 20.00/sFr. 28.00

Recommended prices – alterations reserved

Philip Freneau (1752–1832) was one of the first Americans to gain wide recognition as a writer. He is generally remembered as the «father of American poetry,» but his prose writings have not always received the attention they deserve. As the editor of three important papers in the late 18th century (*The National Gazette*, *The Jersey Chronicle*, and *The Time-Piece and Literary Companion*) and as a contributor to many others, Freneau produced a large number of political and literary essays.

The «Tomo Cheeki Essays», which were published in 1795 and in 1797, constitute an excellent excample of Freneau's prose work. These pseudo-autobiographical accounts of an Indian visiting a city of the Whites are based upon the model of the European «oriental tale,» while simultaneously incorporating American subject matter. The essays are representative of a decisive period of American literary history, since they reveal both Freneau's indebtedness to European culture and his role in the process of overcoming this indebtedness in the beginning creation of an independent national literature. The present edition provides the first complete and separate modern collection of the essays, which gives the reader an opportunity to get acquainted with an important example of early American prose writing that has been virtually inaccessible up to now.

PETER LANG PUBLISHING, INC.
62 West 45th Street
USA – New York, NY 10036